SEAN O'FAOLAIN
A Study of the Short Fiction

Also available in Twayne's Studies in Short Fiction Series

Sherwood Anderson: A Study of the Short Fiction by Robert Allen Papinchak
Donald Barthelme: A Study of the Short Fiction by Barbara L. Roe
Samuel Beckett: A Study of the Short Fiction by Robert Cochran
Jorge Luis Borges: A Study of the Short Fiction by Naomi Lindstrom
Elizabeth Bowen: A Study of the Short Fiction by Phyllis Lassner
Kay Boyle: A Study of the Short Fiction by Elizabeth S. Bell
Truman Capote: A Study of the Short Fiction by Helen S. Garson
Raymond Carver: A Study of the Short Fiction by Ewing Campbell
Willa Cather: A Study of the Short Fiction by Loretta Wasserman
John Cheever: A Study of the Short Fiction by James O'Hara
Robert Coover: A Study of the Short Fiction by Thomas E. Kennedy
Stephen Crane: A Study of the Short Fiction by Chester Wolford
Andre Dubus: A Study of the Short Fiction by Thomas E. Kennedy
F. Scott Fitzgerald: A Study of the Short Fiction by John Kuehl
John Gardner: A Study of the Short Fiction by Jeff Henderson
William Goyen: A Study of the Short Fiction by Reginald Gibbons
Graham Greene: A Study of the Short Fiction by Richard Kelly
Ernest Hemingway: A Study of the Short Fiction by Joseph M. Flora
Henry James: A Study of the Short Fiction by Richard A. Hocks
Franz Kafka: A Study of the Short Fiction by Allen Thiher
Bernard Malamud: A Study of the Short Fiction by Robert Solotaroff
Katherine Mansfield: A Study of the Short Fiction by J. F. Kobler
Gabriel García Márquez: A Study of the Short Fiction by Harley D. Oberhelman
Flannery O'Connor: A Study of the Short Fiction by Suzanne Morrow Paulson
Liam O'Flaherty: A Study of the Short Fiction by James M. Cahalan
Grace Paley: A Study of the Short Fiction by Neil D. Isaacs
Edgar Allan Poe: A Study of the Short Fiction by Charles E. May
V. S. Pritchett: A Study of the Short Fiction by John J. Stinson
J. D. Salinger: A Study of the Short Fiction by John Wenke
William Saroyan: A Study of the Short Fiction by Edward Halsey Foster
Irwin Shaw: A Study of the Short Fiction by James R. Giles
Isaac Bashevis Singer: A Study of the Short Fiction by Edward Alexander
John Steinbeck: A Study of the Short Fiction by R. S. Hughes
Peter Taylor: A Study of the Short Fiction by James Curry Robison
Robert Penn Warren: A Study of the Short Fiction by Joseph R. Millichap
Edith Wharton: A Study of the Short Fiction by Barbara A. White
Tennessee Williams: A Study of the Short Fiction by Dennis Vannatta
William Carlos Williams: A Study of the Short Fiction by Robert Gish
Virginia Woolf: A Study of the Short Fiction by Dean Baldwin

Twayne's Studies in Short Fiction

Gordon Weaver, General Editor
Oklahoma State University

Sean O'Faolain
Used by permission of the Irish Times

SEAN O'FAOLAIN

A Study of the Short Fiction

Pierce Butler
Bentley College

TWAYNE PUBLISHERS · NEW YORK
Maxwell Macmillan Canada · Toronto
Maxwell Macmillan International · New York Oxford Singapore Sydney

Twayne's Studies in Short Fiction Series, No. 50

Copyright © 1993 by Twayne Publishers

Twayne Publishers
Macmillan Publishing Company
866 Third Avenue
New York, New York 10022

Maxwell Macmillan Canada, Inc.
1200 Eglinton Avenue East
Suite 200
Don Mills, Ontario M3C 3N1

Library of Congress Cataloging-in-Publication Data

Butler, Pierce.
    Sean O'Faolain : a study of the short fiction / Pierce Butler.
        p.   cm.—(Twayne's studies in short fiction ; no. 50)
    Includes bibliographical references and index.
    ISBN 0-8057-0860-X
    1. O'Faolain, Sean, 1900–   —Criticism and interpretation.
    2. Ireland in literature. 3. Short story. I Title. II. Series.
    PR6029.F3Z594   1993
    823′.912—dc20   93-18676
                                                              CIP

10 9 8 7 6 5 4 3 2 1

Printed in the United States of America

For my parents
John and Maisie Butler

Contents

Preface

Sean O'Faolain died at his home in Dublin on 20 April 1991, at the age of 91. The publication of *The Collected Stores of Sean O'Faolain* by Atlantic-Little, Brown in 1983 reveals the magnitude of his achievement in the genre during the 50 years since the publication of his first collection in 1932. The volume includes 84 published and six previously unpublished stories; to read them chronologically is to see how O'Faolain charts the development of modern Ireland. The title of Denis Donoghue's review—"Ireland and Its Discontents"—aptly describes O'Faolain's enterprise.[1]

But if O'Faolain's subject matter is predominantly Irish, there is nothing provincial about his sensibility. Like Joyce—though from a radically different perspective—he sets out to discover the universal in Irish experience, and his best stories transcend the limitations of milieu. If Joyce is the émigré writer par excellence, the angry young man who uses the force of his disgust with his predecessors to propel himself into exile, O'Faolain is his stay-at-home counterpart, who feels the constraints of Ireland no less keenly, but manages nevertheless to turn them to good account in his work. Though there are resemblances between Joyce's *Dubliners* and O'Faolain's *A Purse of Coppers*—both are collections of stories pervaded by a sense of futility—in his later work O'Faolain moves towards an acceptance of himself and his origins that the more nomadic and acerbic Joyce did not achieve.

For O'Faolain, Chekhov is a more congenial exemplar. Like the Russian, O'Faolain's interests are broad: he writes about all classes and professions of Irish society—peasants, priests, businessmen, politicians, civil servants, doctors—and depicts the various types of the Irish character, but with the important reservation that "Ireland is worth my attention only when it is the world."[2]

O'Faolain was a writer who engaged his society simultaneously on a number of fronts. His early works fell foul of the Irish Censorship Board, but as founder and editor of the prestigious Irish journal *The Bell* he spoke out against prejudice and narrow-mindedness wherever he found it and did not shrink from confronting the powerful clergy. Elected to the Irish Academy of Letters on the strength of his first collection of stories,

xi

he established the standards for the generation of writers who grew up in the shadow of Yeats and the Irish Renaissance. In an attempt to understand the forces that shaped Ireland, he wrote a number of imaginative biographies of historical figures, most notably, of Hugh O'Neill and Daniel O'Connell. In addition to three collections of stories, he produced three novels and a play during his first decade of literary activity. He was a writer seeking his place and his form.

No doubt his prodigious output in a number of different genres enabled him to make certain critical artistic decisions. He was dissatisfied with his novels; after 1940 he published only one more. He withdrew from *The Bell* and turned to literary criticism, producing studies of the short story and the novel. He rediscovered Italy, which became the subject of two marvelous travel books, and he returned to the U.S. to lecture at Princeton. His widening interests began to be reflected in his stories, which showed an increasing technical control coupled with a gently ironic detachment from his subjects.

While O'Faolain's best stories are virtually unrivaled, he does not display the interest in technical innovation that motivated writers like Hemingway. Declan Kilberd points out that O'Faolain was "strategically poised between the folk and the literary tradition."[3] While the Irish folk tale has not been successfully adapted to the modern short story form, the oral heritage of story telling and the rural culture in which it was rooted have helped nurture the literary tradition. O'Faolain was acutely aware of his heritage and consciously drew his inspiration from it. At first, this is evident in O'Faolain's romantic use of the Irish landscape. As his stories become more tightly focused, he exhibits the story teller's delight in anecdote and in the framing of a story within a story. In his later work, one hears quite clearly the voice of the story teller drawing the reader into an intimate relationship. It is an urbane and knowing voice, to be sure, but it observes conventions analogous to the oral practitioner's confidential manner and verbal flourishes. Above all, O'Faolain wants to tell a good story—and to do so in an intimate and engaging manner.

A typical O'Faolain character is the eccentric who by virtue of exceptional sensibility or intelligence is unfit to become a functioning member of society. Many of his early characters come to grief in the repressive atmosphere of the new Irish state; they kick briefly against the pricks and then subside in quiet resignation. In the later stories, the environment is no less constraining, but O'Faolain allows his characters access to "moments of being" that briefly illuminate their struggles. If they continue to be subject to the hazards of living, there is no longer a sense that an unfavorable outcome is predetermined. The range of possibilities has been expanded, and although there are no guarantees, O'Faolain's eccentrics frequently come to terms with themselves or their struggle against a recalcitrant world. As John Hildebidle puts it, "O'Faolain's early fiction exists within a world that is, if not always truly horrible, then at least grim and threatening, and yet characters find, or try to find, moments of joy; the world of the later fiction seems considerably less dark, considerably more full of human connection rooted in knowledge and emotion, but it is hardly a world without suffering."[4]

The epigraph of *The Short Story*,[5] O'Faolain's 1951 study of the form, is from Flaubert's letters: "The secret of masterpieces lies in the concordance between the subject and the temperament of the author." For O'Faolain, this "concordance" is of paramount importance; it dictates the writer's subject and even a suitable style and technique. O'Faolain is interested in writers like Zola who develop a theory of art and try to realize its implications in their work. But he does not think much of the products of Zola's naturalism—and he would not dream of allowing his own work to be governed by theoretical considerations. He does not experience any abstract dissatisfaction with the technical resources he inherited from Chekhov and Maupassant.

The short stories of George Moore and James Joyce exert a more immediate influence, and it seems inevitable that O'Faolain would adopt many of their themes. Moore's collection of stories *The Untilled Field* and his novel *The Lake* treat the inhabitants of rural Ireland in a way that fascinated the young O'Faolain. The theme of the exceptional individual at odds with his environment is common to both O'Faolain and Moore, but O'Faolain is more sympathetic in his treatment of peasants and priests; the bitterness and satire of *The Untilled Field* are generally absent from O'Faolain's work.[6] O'Faolain admires Joyce "as a writer who successfully used naturalistic techniques to achieve effects that were well beyond the usual objectives of naturalism" (Bonaccorso, 114), but in his own work he usually limits himself to giving naturalism a poetic flavor. O'Faolain's "moments of being" may owe something to Joyce's concept of epiphany, but they allow his characters access, however briefly, to a more expansive consciousness, whereas in *Dubliners* the revelations experienced by Joyce's characters are more often than not moments of shame or humiliation.

What O'Faolain says about the technique of the short story is what any established writer must say to a novice. He emphasizes what the form requires: readily understood conventions, economy of characterization, compression of plot. He has a personal preference for an allusive language that allows the writer of short stories to achieve by suggestion what the novelist has leisure to depict. He admires the compression of stories like Hemingway's, but when all is said, he does not aspire to emulate the moderns. In spite of his interest in form, he is really more concerned with the requirements of his subject. Or perhaps it would be fairer to say that his material most frequently requires a discursive and expansive narrative, by turns precise and allusive, the loquacious and intimate manner of the traditional storyteller.

Acknowledgments

I am grateful to Curtis Brown for permission to quote extensively from *The Collected Stories of Sean O'Faolain* (Boston: Atlantic-Little, Brown, 1983).

I wish to thank the staff of Baker Library, Bentley College, Waltham, MA, for their advice and assistance, and my wife, Susan Holbert, for her support and encouragement with this, as with all my projects.

Part 1

THE SHORT FICTION

The Personal Struggle

Sean O'Faolain was born John Whelan in 1900 in Cork, Ireland's second city. His father, Denis Whelan, was a member of the Royal Irish Constabulary whose allegiance was to the British Crown; this put him at odds with his son, who took the nationalist side in Ireland's struggle for independence. Both of his parents grew up on farms, but having been transplanted to the city, they espoused the middle-class values of education and social advancement. The first stage of O'Faolain's literary journey involved a return to his rural origins as a source of inspiration.

The family lived on Half Moon Street, close to the stage door of the Cork Opera House, and the artists who performed there came as lodgers to the house. As he notes in *Vive Moi!*,[7] his imaginative autobiography, O'Faolain's earliest memories are bound up with the stage: he met the ghost of Hamlet's father in his own kitchen and spent long hours watching the comings and goings at the stage door. A performance of Lennox Robinson's *Patriots* by the Abbey Theater had a profound influence on the idealistic young boy. In recognizing on the stage the life of his mother's family in County Limerick, he discovered that art could make use of the materials of everyday life. He also encountered the reality of a living resistance to British rule that had hitherto existed for him only in the idealized gestures of historical patriots.

Religion was a powerful force in his life. In his autobiography, he recalls the superstition of an old shawlie who approached a statue of the Virgin in a local church to apply her spittle to its wonder-working foot and thence to her "eyes, nose, lips, throat, and heart" (*VM*, 18). But though he repudiates "the delicate-mindedness, or over-protectiveness, or mealy-mouthedness . . . of the Irish Church" (*VM*, 21) in its attitude to sexuality, it leaves its mark upon him, as his embrace of Catholicism in later life clearly shows.

For O'Faolain the discovery of the life of the countryside and the Irish language was a turning point. As a boy he looked forward to visiting his relations in rural Limerick and Laois, and as a young man he spent his summers in the West, studying the Irish language and delighting in a society and an environment that seemed to him more essential and vivifying than Cork city.

He attended University College Cork, where he read his way methodically through an inadequate library. He describes his professor of English as "a man who had traveled to the Land of Literature . . . and come back glowing, stuttering, incoherent, but so obviously fired that his listeners . . . felt that he really had been there and that it might be worth their while to go too" (*VM*, 165). When he suggested to the librarian that the novels of Zola be added to the collection, his suggestion was greeted with amazement and incomprehension. His final judgment on Cork was that, "No intellectual or artist . . . could thrive there unless he got out of it frequently for refreshment" (*VM*, 167).

But the struggle for independence intervened. During the Anglo-Irish War of 1919–1921, O'Faolain took up arms, though he was not called upon to shoot anyone and came under fire only once. After the truce of 1921, he opposed the notorious Treaty which separated six northern counties from the rest of Ireland. He took the anti-Treaty side in the Civil War that followed, during which he first made bombs in Cork city and West Cork and later acted as director of publicity for the Irregulars. The pro-Treaty side emerged victorious, and O'Faolain was disillusioned both by the political turmoil that ensued and by what he regarded as the selling-out of the ideals of the revolution. Armed with a scholarship to Harvard, he left Ireland in 1926 with a sense that he might never return.

O'Faolain's intellectual hunger was satisfied in Boston. O'Faolain spent three years in the U.S., married his Irish sweetheart, and traveled as far as Taos, New Mexico, where the imposing soulessness of the landscape impressed upon him that Ireland was his home. He made his way back via London, where with the help of Edward Garnett he published his first book, *Midsummer Night Madness and Other Stories*, in 1932. This book was promptly banned by the Irish Censorship Board, which put its author in the exalted company of Tolstoy, Balzac, Proust, Mann, and Faulkner, but this did not prevent O'Faolain from returning to the land and the people he most wanted to write about. He established himself and his family in a house in the Wicklow mountains at a convenient distance from Dublin and devoted himself to what was to become a life-long study of the problem of the Irish writer at home. The fruits of this study are to be found in his fiction, his biographies of Irish historical figures, and his numerous commentaries on literary and social conditions.

O'Faolain has written extensively about the writer's vocation, and he places emphasis on "the personal struggle," the tension between the writer and the circumstances of his personal life, from which must evolve all that is of value in the writer's work. O'Faolain's life was subject to three profound influences: the discovery of the Irish language and rural Ireland, the participation in armed struggle, and religion. Each of these influences made a deep impression, but it was only by revisiting and reevaluating them that he came to define his mature attitude. Thus the process of thought that informs his work is continually turning back upon itself to review familiar ground.

O'Faolain saw his parents as uprooted peasants, caught in the rat race of the city, ceaselessly yearning toward middle-class respectability. But they retained a nostalgia for their rural origins and brought their children back to the countryside for vacations. O'Faolain describes his first experience of his mother's native County Limerick: "I was with the ages. I was where nothing ever changes, where everything recurs . . . Habit and custom ruled here. It was a place breathing its own essence. Nothing was imposed, nothing made, everything grew as softly as the morning light through the blind. Here there was no up W. Road and down Saint L., no watch-your-step, no for-God's-sake-mind-who-is-behind-you, nothing except Nothing—the lake, a road, a path, a spring well tasting of iron, the swish of a scythe, a rock to lie on" (*VM*, 78–79). This experience was intensified when as a young man he began to study the Irish language and, under the influence of Eileen Gould, his future wife, to spend the summer months in West Cork where Irish was still the language of everyday life. Irish became for O'Faolain "a symbol of the larger freedom to which we were all groping" (*VM*, 134), for he was beginning to be influenced by the nationalist aspirations of the time that reached a climax in the abortive 1916 Rising. He changed his name to its Irish equivalent, and felt he had discovered in West Cork a "Free Country," the antithesis of everything that was Cork city. Looking back upon this period in *Vive Moi!* O'Faolain finds that he was seeking a new Ireland rooted in rural traditions and in the Irish language. He concludes regretfully that this ambition no longer interests his countrymen:

> Nowadays, the learning of Irish has lost this magical power to bind hearts together. It has lost its symbolism, is no longer a mystique . . .

Today we are not in the least concerned with translating the aspirations of those days into reality . . . there has been a shift of ambition. Then we foresaw the new Ireland as a rich flowering of the old Ireland, with all its old simple ways, pieties, values, traditions. Only the old men went on thinking like this . . . The younger men . . . want a modernized country, prosperity, industrialization, economic success. These ambitions have, for years, been demolishing the bridge with the past, stone by stone, until, inevitably, the Irish language, which is the keystone of the arch, will fall into the river of time. With it the life procession from the past into the present will cease. (*VM*, 141–42)

Many of O'Faolain's early stories draw their inspiration from this yearning for the past and from the life and landscape of the West; the title story of his first collection, "Midsummer Night Madness," opens with a description of a young man's ecstatic escape from the city. Nostaglia also comes to the surface in the 1962 collection *I Remember! I Remember!* in which most of the stories have to do with the relationship between past and present. In fact, O'Faolain repudiates the present as a fit subject for fiction; his experience had to "settle down"—to become the past—before it could be of use to the writer. But this relationship between past and present is not a simple one, and it is never static, never a matter of a once-for-all choice. The ongoing conflict is evident when he expresses the fear in *Vive Moi!* that he has squandered his youth in the West, talking a now-dead language with old men, and dreaming about a mythical Ireland. But his literary journey has been a process of sorting out what he can take with him from what he must abandon:

Let me drag myself free of that dreamworld, that drunk-world, that heavenworld to try to look at it lucidly, now that it has left me and left all of us, sinking deep into the sea like a drowned bell, tolling more and more faintly as it sways downwards, to be heard in our day only by specially tuned ears like those sonic finders that yachtsmen use to take deep-sea soundings. Its gift was lovely, equivocal, dangerous and ultimately exhaustible. . . . While I was in our Free Country I had no wish to think of any other. In that vast, shapeless, indivisible sea of timeless youth and age my being became an absorbent spirit rather than a perceiving intelligence. (*VM*, 141–44)

Back in Cork, O'Faolain discovered an historical and more congenial city in the colorful stories of Eileen Gould's father. He developed an affection for the city evident in his novel *Bird Alone*. In retrospect, a critical question preoccupies him: whether the precocious young man should flee the provincialism of his birthplace—and whether or not he can safely return once he has acquired a thicker skin of culture to shield him from its stultifying influence. O'Faolain concludes that "One may return with less danger" (*VM*, 166), compares himself unfavorably to the "absurdly precocious" Joyce, and identifies with Hawthorne, Hardy, and Faulkner. His account of Cork and its "damp, dark, miasmic valley" (*VM*, 155) is pervaded by ambivalence: love of the city's traditions and historical associations, embarrassment at its cultural pretensions, fear of its provincialism—and relief for having escaped! But he concedes that, like Joyce, his native city has left an indelible mark upon him.

His flight from Cork and from Ireland first took him to the United States. Watching the sun set in Taos, New Mexico, he and his wife wondered if such a country could be their home:

> As we talked I suddenly became aware that, by a trick of the light, a last cut-off peak seemed to stand up quite bare and quite alone across the plateau beneath us. The vast range had otherwise withdrawn itself like mountains in a vision; there was not a soul in sight; the dusk was absolutely silent. Even we were oppressed by the silence and ceased talking. There wasn't even the least cry of a bird. It was an immeasurable night. And it wasn't in the least bit impressive—because if those mountains had associations we did not know them; if history—that is, if some sort of purposeful life, other than of missionaries or explorers, ever trod this vastness—it had left no vibrations for either of us . . . We belonged to an old, small, intimate and much-trodden country, where every field, every path, every ruin had its memories, where every last corner had its story. We decided that we could only live in Europe and in Ireland. (*VM*, 311)

This decision, he assures us, was not made "without grave misgivings," but in making it he defined the terms of his personal struggle: how to live in Ireland and write about it without bitterness.

During his first year at University College Cork, O'Faolain was invited to join the Irish Volunteers, a militant nationalist organization that preceded the Irish Republican Army. Drilling in a field outside the city, O'Faolain felt that "some invisible presence had passed over us with a lighted taper, binding us together not only in loyalty and in friendship but in something dearer still that I am not ashamed to call love. In that moment life became one with the emotion of Ireland. In that moment I am sure every one of us ceased to be single or individual and became part of one another, in union, almost like coupling lovers" (*VM*, 172–73). O'Faolain was disillusioned with the Treaty and the Civil War. He felt that, even within the Free State (as the 26 counties of partitioned Ireland were first named), the ideals of the revolution failed to affect everyday life. He blamed "an acquisitive and uncultivated middle class and a rigorous and uncultivated Church" (*VM*, 221), and whereas his first collection of stories reflects the experience of the ecstatic young patriot, his subsequent disillusionment with life in what was for him the inappropriately styled "Free State" began to find expression in his work. But he was wise enough not to persist in a sterile indictment of a society he had chosen for better or for worse, and he began to detach himself from the sources of his anger. He realized that in his first book he had romanticized his resentment, but his attempt to compensate in *A Purse of Coppers* approached the opposite extreme. There had to be a middle ground, and O'Faolain achieved this through his use of humor and irony and through what he calls a "gradual process of life-acceptance" (*VM*, 225). He now views the ideals of the Irish revolution in a new light—through the eyes of the writer: "The artist . . . must express his ideals in human images. If men and women seem to betray his expressed ideal, his first instinct is to be filled with anger against them, thereby inviting an equally angry response. If his ideal has been a practicable ideal, then their anger against him is unreasonable. If his ideal has been impracticable, then his anger against them is not only unreasonable, but is, in actuality, the mark of his own unacknowledged anger with himself for being such a fool as to have asked too much of human nature" (*VM*, 227). The problem of anger presents itself to him in the following terms:

> No man can paint, or write, or do anything fruitful in a state of rage. If, however, the anger of an artist is directed against and held against the very protoplasm of his art, his own people, he is in a terrible danger of quarreling with the very paint on his brush, the plaster in his hand, the words on his tongue, his model on the dais, his own vision of life, his whole being both as man and artist, and there is really little left to him . . . but to become a psychopath, or fall silent, or become an agitator or a prosecutable pamphleteer. (*VM*, 366)

O'Faolain's later work reflects this insight. Ireland remains his subject, but the note of stridency that spoiled some of his early stories is absent. As a mature artist, he combines a love and respect for his material with a healthy skepticism and a ready appreciation of a good joke. He goes forth from his Wicklow retreat to take part in public affairs, but he has found a way to protect the private self that creates art and to live with the division in his own nature.

Catholicism is the third powerful influence acting on O'Faolain. As a young man he still practiced his religion, although he had doubts about a divinity who permits the existence of suffering and evil. The turning point came at the age of 54 when the chance remark of a French priest living in New York revealed to him the possibility of accepting a world in which evil has a place. His Christian sensibility, troubled by the experience of a bloody civil war, is reconciled to religion by the reflection that the fallibility of the human will is the necessary condition for its free and unfettered development. He discovers that "without the fallible human will there could be no divine will, that our weakness is part of His strength, that without evil there could be no life, that without the humanity of sinful man the whole of God's creation would fall into as fine a dust as a meringue crushed in a cook's fist" (*VM*, 231–32). If the flaws in the design of human life are divinely ordained, this has implications for the role of the artist. O'Faolain's dual acceptance of the ways of man and God leads him to the view that we fulfill ourselves completely as individuals only at moments. It is the artist's business to identify and give form to these moments. As he puts it in his autobiography he has tried to understand

> what flaws in the intricate machinery of human nature keep it from fulfilling itself wholly, from achieving complete integrity other than in moments as brief, if one compares them with the whole span of a human life, as a lighthouse blink. I would, then, in my late life-acceptance, embracing as much as I had the courage to embrace of all of life's inherent evil and weakness, try to write, however tangentially about those moments of awareness when we know three truths at one and the same moment: that life requires of each of us that we should grow up and out whole and entire, that human life of its nature intricately foils exactly this, and that the possibility of wholeness is nevertheless as constant and enormous a reality as the manifold actuality of frustration, compromise, getting caught in some labyrinth, getting cut short by death. (*VM*, 226)

Part 1

The role of the artist, therefore, is not unlike that of a mystic or seer: he is to seek and to frame those rare and elusive moments when we live simultaneously in two worlds, the world of actual limitation and the world of potential freedom. O'Faolain is seeking these moments early and late, and they impart a characteristic tension to his best work.

Revolution and Afterwards

O'Faolain's first collection, *Midsummer Night Madness and Other Stories* (1932), is concerned primarily with the experience of war. The stories are set in the Ireland of "The Troubles," the War of Independence that culminated in the infamous Anglo-Irish Treaty that partitioned the country and the subsequent Civil War, from which the pro-Treaty faction emerged the victors. In spite of the seriousness of his subject, the tone of the stories is predominantly romantic and lyrical, as though O'Faolain were suppressing his anger and disillusionment in favor of a celebration of youth and the rugged beauties of the Irish countryside.

The narrator of the title story[8] is an idealistic young revolutionary sent out of Cork City to censure Stevey Long, a local IRA commandant whose battalion has been mysteriously inactive. His errand is a grim one, but as he cycles out of the city his mind is on other things: the peace and quiet of the countryside and the prospect of encountering the Protestant landowner Henn, a notorious womanizer, whose house Stevey has commandeered. He finds Stevey more interested in the charms of a young tinker girl named Gypsy Gammle than in restraining the nightly excursions of the "Tans," and in a rather Gothic scene he confronts the decrepit Henn in the ruins of his once-grand house. Meanwhile, Stevey rallies his men, burns down the big house across the valley, and threatens Henn with the same fate if he refuses to marry Gypsy who, according to Stevey, is pregnant by the lecherous old man. The story closes with the narrator's report of the ill-matched pair, now man and wife, leaving Cork by train en route to Paris.

The tone of the story is lyrical, especially in its descriptions of nature. As the narrator cycles deeper into the countryside, "Fallen hawthorn blossoms splashed with their lime the dust of the road, and . . . the lilac and the dog-rose, hung with wisps of hay, reached down as if to be plucked" (*CS*, 9). Beneath his wheels, "the lain dust was soft as velvet," the clouds gather "like pale flowers over the inky sky" (*CS*, 13), and after a shower of rain the vegetation seems to "send up its sweetness into the soft wet air" (*CS*, 16). (In fact, since these descriptions are coupled with a portrait of the nubile Gypsy and with intimations of her involvement with Henn and Stevey, the evocation of nature is reminiscent of Hardy's *Tess*.)

There is a leisurely, digressive unfolding of plot that eschews suspense. Henn is introduced in the narrator's reflections before we meet him in person, and indeed the conclusion of the story is anticipated in the narrator's speculation that only tinker women will have anything to do with the aging womanizer. On the face of it, the story reflects the conflicts that found violent expression in the struggle for independence. Henn is representative of a decadent and irresponsible Protestant ascendancy, and the idealistic young narrator confronts him with the principles of the revolution. Henn claims to have been a reforming landlord and blames his decline on the fecklessness of his tenants; he knows the country and its people better than the narrator and his like, who come from the city to incite them to random violence. But the narrator reveals that his parents lived and died on Henn's estate, and this quiets the old man's rage and establishes a bond between them. For all his revolutionary zeal, the young narrator still seems to feel the peasant's impulse to idealize the lord of the manor, and he takes little pleasure in Henn's decline.

Stevey Long is a foil to the narrator and represents the darker side of the struggle for independence. He is the prototype of the gunman (a cold-blooded murderer in a later story in the same collection), uncouth, impulsive, easily distracted, and given to bouts of rage. In his fear of the narrator's censure, he destroys the house of Henn's Protestant neighbours and musters a mob of peasants to march on Henn Hall. The narrator intervenes to prevent violence, but Stevey insists on matching Gypsy and the old man. In the juxtaposition of the tinker woman and the debauched aristocrat there are symbolic echoes of the relationship between Ireland and England. But O'Faolain does not merely use his characters as ciphers; he is also interested in this odd couple for their own sake.

In the most impressive scene of the story, the narrator peers through a window at the half-dressed Gypsy and her decrepit, drooling lover. He censures them both, the girl for her promiscuousness (she may have slept with Stevey too) and Henn for his failure to live up to the ideals of his class. The narrator is ultimately a rather humorless and moralistic revolutionary. If the story has a flaw, it is that the implications of his involvement with the other characters are not fully explored. At the end, O'Faolain's focus is on the bizarre image of the arthritic Henn in Paris with a behatted Gypsy in tow, and we are left to wonder how the narrator's experience has affected his attitude toward the revolution and the class it overthrew.

O'Faolain has created in "Midsummer Night Madness" an opposition between city and country that will be present throughout his work. In spite of his eagerness to be among the fields and hills, the narrator does not leave the city without a backward glance "down through the smoke at the clustered chimney-pots and roofs on whose purples and greens and blues the summer night was falling as gently as dust" (*CS*, 9). Hildebidle finds in his ambivalence "a topographical enactment of a conflict of loyalties and intentions which is at the heart of all of O'Faolain's fiction" (Hildebidle, 131). The narrator's predicament—caught between city and country, past and present, memory and desire—is "a characteristic one for O'Faolain's protagonists" (Hildebidle, 131).

The narrator of "Fugue" is another young Irish rebel on the run from the Black and Tans (British police reinforcements known for their indiscriminate brutality.) Again, he's from the city, and keenly impressed by the sights and sounds of the countryside. He and his comrade find refuge on a farm where the sensitive young man makes much of an exchange of glances with the daughter of the house. His feelings are described in the language of unrestrained romanticism:

> She had looked at me as if we had between us some secret love: not one woman in ten thousand will look so at one man in as many thousand, perhaps not one in all his life, never more than one I would have said a day ago, and now one such had looked at my eyes and I thought at once of the evening glow of the city streets when the sun has gone behind the tallest houses, when the end of the day is near, and the canyon-alleys are suffused with dusk and slow-moving lights: when men waken from the sleep of day and returning in upon themselves think of love, and the darkness where love is, and wander out from the city to the dark fields seeking a secret loneliness for their pain. (*CS*, 52)

However, this romanticism of sentiment is coupled with an attempt to render the dialect of the young man's companion, an uncouth Kerryman impatient with city ways. The farmer conveys the fugitives across a swollen stream on horseback, and the redoubtable Kerryman is almost unseated:

> There was the bloody mare in the middle of the river, I'm not in the habit of horses, you know, a man that was used to horses wouldn't

13

mind, but I wasn't in the habit of them and I never was, and what did
I do and the bloody mare there in the middle of the river, what did I
do, what did I do? The thing I did! What should I *do*, I ask you, but
look down at the flood, so look down at the flood I did. I looked down
and only for the lad got a grip of me I was down. Cripes, I was. I was!
If I would only not look down at the flood, you see, but I looked down,
and by Christ!. (*CS*, 54)

After they survive an encounter with a truckload of Black and Tans
and gain the security of the mountains, the narrator begins to come under
the influence of his surroundings, and the mood of the story becomes
philosophical:

We were come to a little lowflung wood of birch and rowan, the silver
bark peeling black stripes horizontally from the birch, the red berries
of the rowan wind-blown on its delicate branches. Grey rocks covered
the interstices of the trees and the sun fell sometimes on the rock to
warm the cold color: a stream twisted through the rough ground and its
sound was soft and bass . . . Now sloth of mind, as sometimes
before, drew down my heart to the beauty of this life, and in this little
birdless wood, I began to dream. . . . There is an owl in the Celtic
fable who had seen each rowan as a seed upon a tree, and its length
seven times fallen to the earth and seven times over raised in leaf . . .
Such an owl called out of the dusk at me and its cry filled me with age
and the peace that comes when we feel the wheels of the passing years
turn so slowly it is almost complete rest. (*CS*, 55–56)

The allusion to the owl in this passage is significant. The idea of an
individual who outlives generations by assuming the forms of animals is
a common one in Irish mythology; what usually happens is that the
individual assumes human form again after the lapse of thousands of
years and tells his story to a Christian priest or monk or even to St. Patrick
himself, thus establishing a connection between pagan and Christian
traditions. O'Faolain uses this and other allusions to mythology to broaden
the frame of reference of the story, to suggest a connection between the
confused flight of these two incompetent soldiers and the heroic past of
legend and myth.

The fugitives take refuge from a storm in separate cottages—and the
narrator finds himself alone with the young woman whose glance had so
affected him. The Kerryman is caught off guard and shot in bed, and the
narrator is forced to flee from his courting into the stormy night. He finds

a modicum of shelter in a ruined cottage and curses his lot. But as day breaks and he moves on, he seems far from disheartened: "The dawn moved along the rim of the mountains and as I went down the hill I felt the new day come up around me and felt life begin once its ancient, ceaseless gyre" (*CS*, 64).

The revelation, half way through the narrative, that the Kerryman is fated to die in an ambush, indicates that O'Faolain's intentions have nothing to do with suspense. The plot of the story, which is sufficiently complex (even the narrator wonders how the young woman can have gotten ahead of him after a day's forced march), interests O'Faolain far less than the opportunity to present his characters against the backdrop of the ageless Irish countryside and the cycles of life and death. He chooses his narrator accordingly; the young man is almost morbidly sensitive to his surroundings, by turns romantic and philosophical. At sunset, he sees "the West grow cold and saffron as if the threshers of the morn, reduplicated in valley after valley had blown a storm of corn-sheaves against the falling cape of night" (*CS*, 56). His longing for the girl whom coincidence is about to thrust into his arms prompts him to the following reflection: "What sad weavings the old Weaver of life can think of, as if all will not fray away and moths rise from the eyes of his dears, and all his storms crumble at the end in dust" (*CS*, 58).

There is a tension between this kind of prose and the realism O'Faolain sets himself to achieve through dialogue and observation. Ultimately, the earthy dialect of the Kerryman and the careful description of the country folk going about their immemorial tasks are overwhelmed by O'Faolain's desire to place them in a larger context. The marriage of realism and romanticism is unsuccessful because the narrator must at one and the same time be a character in the story and the embodiment of a universal, omnipotent point of view. Yet this broadening of the point of view gives the story its grandeur. Alone on the wet mountains, the narrator reflects that winter has come. At this point the narrative is interrupted by an Irish nature poem to winter. If the illusion of realism is punctured by the insertion of an anonymous eleventh century lyric, the effect of the poem is to add stature to the narrator, who is elevated to an almost mystical sense of unity with the countryside and the cycles of nature. The device does not belong to the canon of realism, since this unity is not an integral part of the character's experience, but rather something imposed from without by the author. But the lyrical suggestion of an enduring reality underlying the tribulations of war and peace is none the less impressive.

It is instructive to compare this ending with the final paragraph of Frank O'Connor's famous story "Guests of the Nation." Bonaparte, the narrator of this story, is also a member of the IRA. He is obliged to shoot two British prisoners—the guests of the title—with whom he and his comrade Noble had become friendly. The woman referred to in this passage has had her house commandeered by the IRA as a place of confinement for the prisoners:

> Then by God, in the very doorway, she fell on her knees and began praying, and after looking at her for a minute or two Noble did the same by the fireplace. I pushed my way out past her and left them at it. I stood at the door, watching the stars and listening to the shrieking of the birds dying out over the bogs. It is so strange what you feel at times like that that you can't describe it. Noble says he saw everything ten times the size, as though there were nothing in the whole world but that little patch of bog with the two Englishmen stiffening into it, but with me it was as if the patch of bog where the Englishmen were was a million miles away, and even Noble and the old woman, mumbling behind me, and the birds and the bloody stars were all far away, and I was somehow very small and very lost and lonely like a child astray in the snow. And anything that happened me afterward, I never felt the same about again.[9]

Thus O'Faolain's narrator is linked to the cycles of nature and mythology and his blundering about in the dark invested with a heroic quality, whereas O'Connor's is isolated by his sense of guilt from the comforts of religion, from his comrades, from nature. Hildebidle points out that whereas "O'Connor's fictional world is rigorously interior" (Hildebidle, 134n), O'Faolain's characters are subject to an ongoing tension between confinement and escape. Bonaparte is confined by his guilt within the prison of self, whereas O'Faolain's narrator experiences an expansion of the self and the freedom of a momentary unity with nature.

O'Faolain also differs from O'Connor in that—at least in "Fugue" and many of the other stories of his first collection—he is not interested in the rigorous realism of "Guests of the Nation." It may be that O'Faolain's romanticism and the complexity of his allusions are a means of glossing over the sort of shattering experience O'Connor is writing about in a more direct and realistic voice. At this stage of his career, O'Faolain's clear preference is for the Ireland of poetry and myth.

In "The Patriot," the final story in *Midsummer Night Madness*, a move toward a more rigorous realism is evident, and it is probably no coincidence that the subject of the story is disillusionment. The action takes place during the last months of the Irish Civil War. The Irregulars are in disarray, hunted from mountain to mountain by the well-equipped troops of the Free State, and the young rebel Bernard can think only of the summer he has spent with a young woman in the seaside town of Youghal. His path is repeatedly crossed by an older man, Edward Bradley, a schoolteacher and passionate nationalist, who shares his affection for Norah and his commitment to the cause. Bernard and Norah attend a rally at which Bradley speaks "with a terrible passion against England" (*CS*, 146), and they are fired by his enthusiasm.

But Bernard next encounters Bradley at a rowdy and anarchic meeting of the Irregular officers in a little mountain village, and the older man's plea for a continuation of the struggle seems futile and insensitive. Bernard surrenders to the Free-Staters, serves his time in prison, and emerges to marry Norah. They return to Youghal, the scene of their courtship, on their wedding day, and by chance find themselves in a crowd assembled to hear Bradley speak. The old patriot is as passionate as ever, but the couple slip away silently to enjoy their wedding night, symbolically repudiating political passion for married love.

"The Patriot" contains many of the themes of the other stories in the collection—the idealistic young rebel, the heightened sensitivity to nature, the interruption of love by war—but the treatment of these themes is new. Bernard parades his patriotism before Norah on their first meeting and gallantly denounces the Anglo-Irish families of Youghal. When he is forced to flee into the mountains, he forgets her in the rigors of an ineffective guerrilla campaign. But instead of being enraptured by the stark beauty of the landscape like his counterpart in "Fugue," he is all but suffocated by his environment: "The days scarcely existed for him and the weeks flew over his head as unnoticed as birds homing at night, until as a human being he almost ceased to be, enveloped by the countryside as if he were a twig, a stone, an ear of corn" (*CS*, 148). When he suddenly recalls Youghal and Norah, his being revolts against his life on the run in "the cold and naked mountains" (*CS*, 148). He now longs for the city with the same intensity of feeling with which the narrator of "Midsummer Night Madness" longed to escape it: "He could hear the streams swirling down the dark *leaca* and as he listened their roar mingled terror with the desolation of the black silence, and he wished passionately to be away from so lonely and cruel a place" (*CS*, 149).

He thinks of obtaining a loan and a change of clothes so that he can return to the city in safety. The discipline of the guerrillas is on the point

17

of disintegration, and Bernard despises their stupidity and feels sorry for the peasants upon whom they are quartered. While the officers wrangle drunkenly over strategy, he pores over a letter from Norah. The words of a poem he had recited to her come to his mind; as in "Fugue" the narrative is interrupted by poetry, but the poem is addressed to a woman rather than to Nature. Bernard is not insensitive to the charms of Nature, but they act upon him most forcibly in the presence of Norah. In the mountains, he recalls repeatedly the wood near Youghal where he courted her, and the ecstasy of their reunion is inextricably bound up with the coming of spring in Youghal:

> They went about that first day, their wedding day, noticing every-thing with new delight—the spears of green grass shooting through the dead fields, the primroses and the violets clustered near the grey stones in the ditches, the beech-buds swollen red, the patches of hawthorn green lighting the withered hedges. . . . When they lay under an early blossoming blackthorn high above the singing sea and in the long silences of deep love gazed over the empty horizon . . . Bernard felt . . . that if another gull should wheel through the blue air, another distant lamb call out to its dam, their cups of ecstasy must overflow and roll upon the ground. (*CS*, 161)

The coming of nightfall over the harbor distracts Bernard from Bradley's oratory, but whereas the narrator of "Fugue" might have been moved to philosophy, Bernard is a young man on his wedding night, too immersed in the love of his wife for detached reflection.

O'Faolain's advance toward realism is also signaled by a greater em-phasis on dramatic incident. Whereas many of the earlier stories of the collection culminate with the reflections of an isolated character, in "The Patriot" O'Faolain finds a way to dramatize Bernard's choice of love. Standing at the hotel window, the young man sees Bradley's car drive off into the night: his wife calls him from the bed, and he draws down the blind. This is simple, but effective. However, in other places, the story remains dominated by the narrative voice of the author, and this works against clarity of characterization.

The emotion of the lovers is almost invariably conveyed through their sense of place and heightened perception of nature, and even in the final scene Bernard's impressions of Bradley seem to belong to the author rather than the character. The rivalry of the two men for Norah's affection is hinted at but not explored, and O'Faolain ensures that it cannot contribute to the story by revealing the conclusion in the first line. Still, he has made a break with the cloying romanticism of "Midsummer Night Madness" and "Fugue" by abandoning the type of the dreamy, sensitive idealist upon whom these stories are based. "The Patriot" reveals the beginning of a deeper interest in characterization. The philosophical digressions return in later stories, but only after O'Faolain has mastered the devices of the realist.

J. S. Rippier[10] speculates that the style of O'Faolain's early stories has been influenced by the prose of George Moore's *The Untilled Field*, with its long circuitous sentences and summary compression of action and thought. Moore himself was operating under the influence of the French symbolists, with their emphasis on the inner life, and perhaps remembering the story telling tradition of his native place. The style Moore experimented with in stories like "Homesickness" was brought to perfection in his novel *The Lake*, in which the narrative account of the main character's thought processes merges with action and dialogue to form a seamless whole. If O'Faolain's early prose bears a superficial resemblance to Moore's, it is important to note that their goals were different. At this stage of his career, O'Faolain is struggling to find a balance between his lyrical impulse and his interest in the appearance of things. His treatment of the inner life will never be as profound as Moore's—or rather he will chose to write about it in terms of appearances—and he will master the conventions of realism before he learns to use the narrator as story teller as effectively as O'Connor.

The State of Ireland

The stories of *A Purse of Coppers* (1937), written in the aftermath of the Civil War, dwell upon the conflict between Irish eccentrics of various classes and the conservative, narrow-minded atmosphere of the Free State. The romanticism verging on nature mysticism of the first collection is replaced by an unsparing description of the frustration of life in provincial towns. During the two years he spent in the United States, O'Faolain had the opportunity to distance himself from Ireland, to study and marry, and to distill the emotions of war. These emotions are not evident in *Midsummer Night Madness*, where feeling is generally subject to style, but they are found in this second collection in O'Faolain's vision of Ireland as "a broken world" that almost invariably dooms his characters to failure.

The cultural backdrop against which the stories are to be understood is given dramatic form in "A Broken World." In a railway carriage traveling through a snowy landscape, an embittered priest expounds to a bored young man and a peasant his theory that the new Ireland lacks unity and direction without the civilizing influence of the Anglo-Irish gentry, who have fled to England and abandoned their estates. His parish, though impoverished, once sustained an aristocracy, and in spite of its shortcomings, this arrangement is preferable to the dereliction of the estates and the flight from the land. The peasant, unable to understand the priest's theory, seems proof of the demoralization of his race, while the young man, though he rebels against this gloomy nostalgia, cannot "deny to the wintry moment its own truth, and that under that white shroud, covering the whole of Ireland, life was lying broken and hardly breathing" (*CS*, 173).

The story is a little too programmatic to be effective. O'Faolain still requires his characters to articulate his themes rather than embedding theme in the action of the story. One is also surprised to encounter this nostalgia for colonialism after the impassioned tones of *Midsummer Night Madness*. However, in reading the stories that follow, it becomes apparent that O'Faolain's subject is the spiritual paralysis that follows revolution. The high ideals of revolution have been diluted or absorbed into the intractability of daily life. Worst of all, from the point of view of the revolutionaries of *Midsummer Night Madness*, the excitement of armed struggle has given way to the unrelenting and ultimately more demanding struggle with fate and circumstance.

Pat Lenihan, the hero of "A Born Genius," exemplifies this struggle. He is an eccentric Corkonian, a clerk in a vinegar factory, possessed of a passable tenor voice and a penchant for unworkable projects, dubbed genius by his uncomprehending peers. He has botched the monument he carved for his sister's grave by misspelling her name, and when we first encounter him he is engaged in building a boat—the symbol of his vague longing to escape from provincial obscurity. This longing crystallizes upon the person of Trixie Flynn, an old flame of Pat's, who has escaped to Milan and operatic stardom, only to return to dissatisfaction with her husband and the lesser eminence of the Cork Opera House. Inspired by her example Pat sets out for New York, where his father, who deserted the family when Pat was a boy, has hopes of establishing him as a tenor. The New World fills Pat with hope; after the confinement of Cork, he finds Ninth Avenue beautiful: "a dirty, paper-strewn cobbled street, darkened and made raucous by an overhead railway" (*CS*, 248). But Lenihan senior postpones their meeting, and when it finally occurs Pat learns that his father has set up another ménage and will never return to be reunited with his mother. This discovery cripples his ambition and reveals the inflexibility of his character. He turns a deaf ear to his father's entreaties, and it is not until he has fled to Cork that it occurs to him to pity the old man. At home, the city impresses him all the more strongly with its provinciality and pretensions:

> This rat-eaten place still had, he thought bitterly, as he walked through its tawdry front streets whose finery was only the thickness of a brick, and into its warehouse back streets that looked as if they had been rusting and crumbling for centuries, all the mannerisms and unconscious humour ascribed to it by the sniggering Levers and Prouts and Thackerays of a hundred years ago. With a kind of sour joy he began to roam about the city . . . associating his own misery with the shades of the Spensers and the Warbecks and the Walters—for he refused to ally even his thoughts with the people themselves—the Dukes and Earls and Lords-Lieutenants and Secretaries whose petty glories were the only ones the place had ever seen. Everywhere he went he sought with deliberate malice for the signs of decayed grandeur—streets of Georgian houses full of cheap shops, a puny

21

bridge called after Wellington, a wide street dubbed a Square and given to Nelson, a horse-trough presented to a Berwick, a wretched slum street to the whole House of Hanover, and every sooty, mud-deep quay partitioned off here to a Grenville, or a Wandesford, or a Camden, or a Lancaster, a George, a Charlotte, an Albert. Every exiled down-at-heel sighing for St James's and Pall Mall, with their flea-bitten servants and tarnished finery, had been offered the immortality of their names on the walls of a jakes in this city of exile. (CS, 254)

His trip to the New World has soured Cork forever. Lenihan thinks of himself as a misfit and identifies with the colonists and adventurers for whom Cork was a "city of exile." He seeks out Trixie, and for a while they find consolation in each other. But even such a modest affair as theirs cannot avoid censure in small-town society, and when their feeling manifests itself in a passionate duet on the opera house stage, a disapproving cleric and a jealous husband shorten Trixie's leash. Pat is left alone with his boat, which proves, predictably enough, to be unseaworthy. In the final scene, reminiscent in its bleakness of the conclusion of Joyce's "A Painful Case," he sits in his tiny house among the narrow lanes of the city slums with his hands resting on the keys of a cheap piano. Like Duffy in Joyce's story, he is listening for a sound that will tell him he is not alone—but in vain.

O'Faolain is a gentler writer than Joyce. He treats his characters with a kindly rather than a sardonic humor, and at times his narrators seem to plead with the reader for a similar indulgence. The narrative voice of "A Born Genius" is largely that of a participant in the provincial society Pat Lenihan comes to despise; it treats Pat's brother, the drunken, cross-eyed Flyer, with indulgence, records the slum's assessment of Trixie Flynn ("a born guttersnipe"), and in general reflects the values of small-town society without comment. Yet when Pat returns from his fruitless sojourn in New York, the scales fall from his eyes, and he sees the pretensions of this society as an outsider. Revealing a knowledge of history perhaps not entirely in character, he turns on his own people with an extraordinary ferocity and identifies himself with all the English who were ever unhappy in Cork and longed for a more cosmopolitan life in London. The conclusion of his abortive affair with Trixie serves to confirm his disaffection.

There is more than an echo of Joyce in this devastating depiction of provincial life. The nets flung at the soul are not those of language, nationalism, and religion, but the incomprehension of ambition, the stern disapproval of passion, and the threadbare amusements that take the place of culture, all of which stifle life and hope.

The narrative voices of Joyce's *Dubliners* display more detachment than O'Faolain's. When Joyce's characters themselves narrate, they do so in a language that reflects the emotion of the author rather than the idiom of the street (Rippier, 46). The effect of this is to make the reader aware of the distance between the author and his subjects. By contrast, the participation of O'Faolain's narrative voices in their milieu tends to minimize this effect. O'Faolain has moved his center of gravity from the overwrought consciousness of the rebels of *Midsummer Night Madness* to a more mediate position, but he will never share Joyce's determination to project himself beyond his own culture in order to take the scalpel to it from without.

O'Faolain is also moving toward a more accomplished realism—but by fits and starts. The opening chapter of the story appears to tell us all we need to know about Lenihan in an efficient and dramatic way; his character is presented through the eyes of the befuddled Flyer and his cronies. However, the profluence of the story is later interrupted by the disclosure that Pat has a father and that the father has deserted the family. Lenihan's pursuit of his father in New York is handled delicately, and yet O'Faolain seems to shrink from the emotion of it, disclosing almost in passing the poignant detail that "for all the four months he [Lenihan] was in New York his father had watched him coming out of the archway of the Seminary in the morning and going in, often very late at night, getting no more in return for his patient vigil than the briefest glance at his son's face" (*CS*, 249). The father's steadfast affection for his son and the wreck of his hopes are very movingly rendered, but O'Faolain chooses to omit the final pathetic scene. The narrative shifts back and forth uneasily between a leisurely exposition characteristic of *Midsummer Night Madness* and dialogue, as if the author were not quite sure where to place his emphasis.

However, the burden of the plot's development is carried by dramatic scenes, and Lenihan and Trixie Flynn emerge as unique and idiosyncratic characters who are not overshadowed by the author's larger design. Nature is hardly a presence in this story, though when Lenihan finds consolation in the changing of the season, a description of the "loveliness of the country encroaching on . . . the empty town" is used to good effect.

For O'Faolain during this period, Ireland is a divided and broken world. Past is sundered from present, priest from flock, the gentleman from his estate. It is a society dislocated by revolution, and all human relationships are affected. O'Faolain explores some of these dislocations in "Discord." The plot of this story is a simple one. A young married couple, honeymooning in Dublin, pay a duty call upon a priest. The priest reminds them of the history of the city, which interests the husband, and shows them the crypt of his church, which frightens the banal but shrewd young wife. When they are alone, they repair this little breach by making the priest the butt of their jokes. Their insincerity and the priest's embarrassment in their company mirror a society in which relations between youth and age, between the faithful and their priestly mentors, have become confused.

The priest, Father Peter, is a lonely bibliophile immersed in the lore of his city parish. He senses the obligation the couple are under and leads them immediately to the window of his room to view the city. In his enthusiasm for the prospect—"It's wonderful there at night . . . with all the lights. It's like Paris from Montmartre." (*CS*, 279)—Father Peter forgets his discomfort, and the young man is moved. But the girl is offended by the slum-houses and turns the conversation back to conventional pleasantries. This is her function throughout the story. Whenever her husband shows signs of responding to the priest's enthusiasm for the life of the mind and the city, her trivialities come between them.

The husband fears being cut off from life and culture: "Everyone living in the country has that feeling sometimes" (*CS*, 280). In response, Father Peter complains of his work. True he meets people, but "it's always a certain kind of people. Sad stories. Rotten stories. Down-and-out stories. Always the same. Drunks, paupers, prostitutes—ach!" (*CS*, 280). The girl again deflects the conversation. ("You have a lot of books?") The priest tells them that the poet James Clarence Mangan wrote his poems in the room, and the young man, excited by the association, begins to quote from Mangan. Things are getting a little too serious and high-falutin' for the girl. The priest notices her silence and suggests a tour of the crypt.

The couple are now treated to a history of the site and the people buried there. They're both a little taken aback by rotting coffins and dark gloomy vaults; the girl complains of the heat, and the youth feigns bravado. The priest insists on taking them out on the town. While they wait for him, they find themselves sobered: "They had come upon one of those moments of life when, like the winter butterflies in the high corners, they felt the hurt of cold" (*CS*, 284). They go through the motions and make merry with the priest, but are glad to be shut of him and make fun of him behind his back. They repair to the marriage bed, and Father Peter is left to his books, his dreams of history, and the sordid exchanges of his parish.

This is a well-constructed story, and its point is clear enough. However, the point of view remains somewhat diffuse, a consequence perhaps of O'Faolain's concern with the dilemma his characters represent rather than with the characters themselves. The girl is more shrewd than she's given credit for; in retrospect, it seems superfluous, if not inaccurate, to suggest "she did not guess that in his [her husband's] mind that image of a vast Dublin, growing and decaying, was still dilating like a smoke in wind" (*CS*, 280). She knows her man—and effectively stifles in him any yearnings that might prove troublesome. O'Faolain brings husband's and wife's points of view together in their shared consciousness of "the hurt of cold." While the image of "the winter butterflies in the high corners" is a fine one and the coincidence of their impressions conveys their solidarity in the face of all the priest represents, the husband's repudiation of larger ambitions is unexpected and has not been prepared for during the crypt scene.

It is undoubtedly part of O'Faolain's intention to show the irrelevance of the priest's interests to the lives of the couple, but this fact is emphasized at the expense of character, and in the end we do not know how the young man has reconciled himself to a prosaic wife or if the priest senses he has made himself objectionable. "A grand girl, Frankie, boy," is Father Peter's spoken judgment upon the girl; O'Faolain's is contained in the story's final sentence: "However, nobody but she saw the joke, and even she, in her wisdom, as women do with their wisdom, never thought about it when she recalled it, as she never forgot it when it had long passed out of her silly little head" (*CS*, 285). Ambiguity apart, this authorial comment is entirely superfluous; we already know precisely what we should think of the girl. O'Faolain has devices of great subtlety at his disposal. "Discord" represents an attempt to operate within the conventions of a more scrupulous realism than he has previously attempted, but understandably enough he cannot yet quite refrain from guiding the reader's judgment in ways that seem redundant.

In "Admiring the Scenery," another story from *A Purse of Coppers*, O'Faolain again attempts to define the state of Ireland, this time by presenting us with three characters who represent a particularly Irish range of responses to experience. The story is set in a country railway station; the characters, one a priest and all of them teachers in the Diocesan College of a provincial town, are returning after a day's walk in the country. One of the lay teachers starts a discussion about the ability of the "common people" to appreciate nature and by way of illustration tells the story of a former station master and his frustrated ambition to become a successful singer. The other lay teacher does not see the relevance of the story to the discussion, and the three characters fall silent as the train carries them back to the town.

In his initial description of the characters, O'Faolain makes it plain that they are suffering from the tedium of provincial life, to which they have attempted to reconcile themselves in their different ways. The priest is "a young man, too fat for his years, with drooping lids, puffed lips, and a red face as if he suffered from blood pressure" (*CS*, 194). He has "the appearance of a man who had gone through many struggles and finally solved his problems in a spirit of good-humored regret" (*CS*, 194). He is a fatalist; his situation is thus marginally better than that of the others. Mr. Governey, "a small dark man, with a slim small body and a button of a head and clipped dark moustaches" (*CS*, 195), is a malcontent. He complains about the remoteness of the railway station and refuses to concede that the country people are capable of anything more than a beast-like contentment in the face of the beauty of nature, but he seems to derive some sour pleasure from his complaints.

The central figure in the story, Hanafan, is a type of the artist: "There was nothing resigned about him; his oblong face was blackberry-coloured where he shaved and delicate as a woman's where he did not. His eyes were lined with a myriad of fine wrinkles. They were cranky, tormented eyes, and his mouth was thin and cold and hard" (*CS*, 195). It is Hanafan who initiates the discussion about nature, who quotes from Gray's "Elegy" and from Sir Thomas Browne, and who is finally moved to tears by his own recollections. His is the most unhappy lot of the three: the priest regards him with fatalistic sympathy, Governey with irritated incomprehension.

Hanafan's conviction is that the countryman *can* appreciate nature, "even though he might not know he was doing so at all" (*CS*, 196). To prove his point, he tells the story of the former station master, one Boyhan, a man whose singing voice does not measure up to the strength of his ambitions. Boyhan is a widower; his children have grown and left him. When he is transferred to the lonely station, he continues to aspire to greater things and sings to the passengers of the Dublin trains in the forlorn hope of being discovered by a passing dignitary. Hanafan describes a visit to the station in the company of a friend. The station master entertains them with song, but is carried away with his own emotion and causes them to miss their train. Hanafan and his friend walk home in the night, leaving the old man alone in the station. He claims that the singer's mediocre voice, in the loneliness of the countryside, was a sort of hymn to nature. Governey is puzzled until he notices Hanafan is moved by his own story, whereupon he begins to suspect that Hanafan's friend was a woman and that their romance came to an unhappy end. The priest is obviously in the know, and Governey resolves to get the rest of the story out of him when they are alone. As the trio sit silently in the train, Hanafan is weeping quietly, unnoticed by his companions.

We have here a group of individuals, the singing station master included, frustrated by their environment. The unnamed town in which they live and teach is obviously no place for a man with a desire to make even a modest success of his life. The priest remains because he has been assigned there—and has attained resignation. Governey cannot tear himself away because his temperament requires the constant irritation of complaint, and Hanafan, the character with the best prospect of escaping to the larger world, lingers near the scene of past happiness, his ambition vitiated by his unhappy love affair, finding an expression of his fate in the station master and his pathetic self-deception. The darkness of provincial life is almost unrelieved.

Hanafan attempts to find some consolation in the beauty of the evening and in the possibility of a subtle communication between human beings and nature, but he is an unhappy, frustrated man, and his sensitivity to memories and impressions forms an ironic contrast with the bleakness of his inner life. The only possible solution, O'Faolain seems to suggest, to the predicament of life in Ireland is that of the priest: a good-humored fatalism that inures one against hope.

The device of the "story within a story" is a favorite one of O'Faolain's, especially in his earlier work. It is inadequately handled here, however, because the impact upon Hanafan of what he himself has witnessed is rather vague—and because the reader is left in the dark about Hanafan's love life, along with Governey. O'Faolain has again found a fine image, that of the station master singing to the trainload of indifferent passengers and allowing the train to leave the station before Hanafan and his friend can cross the tracks. But there's no intrinsic connection between this image and the feeling with which Hanafan remembers the evening, except for the purely coincidental: everything he saw that night is colored by his love for his companion and his subsequent regret for the passing of that time. It's hard not to ask with the irascible Governey, "What has all that got to do with admiring the scenery?" (*CS*, 200).

Hanafan claims that the station master "sang to the night" (*CS*, 200). But we already know that the station master had a more utilitarian motive. Is Hanafan trying to assert that the beauty of nature can sometimes compensate for failure and loneliness? Or that love can transfigure a bleak and unromantic landscape? The story explicitly raises these questions, but without providing satisfactory answers.

In discussing this story, Rippier notes a significant change in O'Faolain's methodology, again by means of a comparison with George Moore (Rippier, 75–76). Moore's "Homesickness" is the story of one James Bryden, who lives to regret his desertion of an Irish girl he promised to marry and his decision to make his life in New York. Moore's third person narrator states the essential theme of the story in a single sentence: "There is an unchanging, silent life within every man that none knows but himself, and his unchanging, silent life was his memory of Margaret Dirken."[11] The plot of the story presents Bryden's decision to leave Ireland and leaps ahead to the end of his life in order to describe its ultimate consequences. O'Faolain's method is to put the treatment of his theme into the mouths of his characters and to oblige us to infer Hanafan's inner state from the story he tells about someone else. Unlike Moore, O'Faolain declines to interpret the experience of his character: the result is a story in which action and dialogue must speak for themselves.

The "story within a story" device and a similar theme are more skillfully exploited in "Lady Lucifer," a story from *Teresa and Other Stories* (1947). As in "Admiring the Scenery," there are three characters who embody a range of attitudes toward Irish life. The bank clerk wants to escape from the drudgery of his job in the city and find a rural retreat in which he can devote himself to his writing; the doctor, who has traveled and seen the world, deplores this attitude as *nostalgie de la boue*; the priest is again a confirmed fatalist, resigned to the limitations of Irish society, who calls the attention of his companions to the delights of the countryside. The three are boating in what seems an enchanted landscape:

> The three friends had rowed very slowly down-river—half-floated,
> indeed—seeing only the withered thistles in the fields, cows standing

to their ankles in still water. There was not a speck in the sky. Not
even a bird; as if they had taken shelter from the humming heat in the
pine-forest that rose on one side, dark and cool as a cave. The only
sound they heard for a mile was the fall of water in the canal-lock; and
when they passed through the lock and were lazily poling along the
slim perspective of the canal, everything was again sloth and softness
and sun. The narrow road of canal was a dreaming slip of water. They
were secluded, lost, tucked-away. The world had died. . . . As they
rocked gently along, these two jungles of river-plants undulated
faintly—balsam, golden flags, willow-herbs, coltsfoot, purple loose-
strife: their delicate pungency scented the warm air. Nobody spoke.
(*CS*, 429)

They visit a lock-house, and the doctor persuades the woman of the
house to give them tea. The priest approves the "old and traditional"
way of life of the lock-house woman, but the doctor takes the opportunity to remind the clerk of the rigors of winter in such a place: "Lucas
here imagines he'd like it. You really wouldn't, you know. Anybody like
you with ambition has to live a full life. Anybody with a bit of pride in
him. You'd run out of it in a month" (*CS*, 434). This starts a dispute
between priest and doctor on the meaning of pride. The priest regards it
as the most serious sin, whereas the doctor contends that "there isn't
enough pride of any sort in this country. There's too much damned
humility" (*CS*, 434). To illustrate this claim, the doctor tells the story of
a young nurse in a mental hospital whose fiancé, a former nurse and
returned exile, has a breakdown and is confined under her care. She
gives up her ambition to escape the drudgery of her job and resigns
herself to life as matron of the hospital, where she continues to wear her
deranged lover's engagement ring. It is a grotesque story, and it prompts
the clerk to the fatalistic remark that "life is a divil" (*CS*, 444). He seems
to acknowledge here that the humility engendered by Irish life has crushed
the nurse's ambitions.

O'Faolain is working with the same materials he used in "Admiring
the Scenery," but "Lady Lucifer" is more successful for a number of
reasons. First, the doctor's story clearly illustrates his point about Irish
life, and there is no uncertainty about his attitude to his own experience
or to that of the nurse. He is a confident man of action, in contrast to the
ambivalent and ambiguous Hanafan. Second, O'Faolain makes much
more skillful use of setting here. In "Admiring the Scenery," we are told
the railway station is a "God-forsaken place," and we do not have a

sufficiently clear picture of the setting to understand Hanafan's fascination with it. But the Irish countryside is a much more vivid presence in "Lady Lucifer" and forms a poignant backdrop to the disputation of the characters. It is an idyllic landscape, but O'Faolain is capable in his description of suggesting its remote and soporific qualities: "It is a lost corner, barely coming to life, some dim noise half-heard through sleep, a moth on a window-pane at morning, an occasional barge slowly dud-dudding along the river, disturbing the coots and the wild-flowers with its arrowy wake. The very air of this deep valley seems too heavy to move. Even then a little cloud lay on the tip of the far line of mountains, too exhausted to persist. . . . A heron rose from the island and flapped away in bored sloth into the woods" (*CS*, 430).

Rippier has pointed out the subtle connection between the characteristically Irish humility the doctor deplores and O'Faolain's choice of language (Rippier, 117). As the friends watch a barge recede down the canal, "the river-plants on either side bowed their heads deep into the water and slowly swung upwards again when the arrows had passed on" (*CS*, 444)—as though echoing the nurse's submission to circumstance. We know what we are to think about the Irish countryside here. The doctor has the last word: "Dear God . . . This is heaven! Heaven!" (*CS*, 445). But it seems plain that only his critical detachment enables him to appreciate it. The priest has an unthinking commitment to traditional ways and values, and the unfortunate clerk is caught between a romantic longing for a rural hermitage and a sense of horror at the possible consequences of such isolation.

The lack of resolution of the dispute between doctor and priest is perfectly acceptable here, since the relationships between the characters have been clearly articulated and we do not have to guess at their emotions, as in the case of Hanafan. O'Faolain has more distance on his subject, and he provides the doctor as a foil to the confusion of the clerk and the conservatism of the priest. The story of the nurse tends at times by its length and detail to distract the reader's attention from the three boaters. O'Faolain remains consistently interested in the conventions of storytelling throughout his career, but he does not really make them work for him until he transforms his narrators into traditional storytellers, with all the idiosyncrasies of the breed.

Frank O'Connor frequently makes more adroit use of the "story-within-a story" device. In "The Grand Vizier's Daughters," for example, the story that the father tells his daughters has apparently nothing to do with their lives, but it turns out to be an excuse for the father to accuse one of his daughters of disloyalty and precipitates an emotional crisis for the other. In addition to integrating the character's story fully into the theme of his own story, O'Connor has provided an example of the way in which storytelling is frequently used in contemporary Ireland, as a form which allows the expression of emotions too highly charged to be communicated directly.

In "Kitty the Wren," the prejudices of rural Ireland are viewed from the outside, through the eyes of a French sailor who comes ashore in a small Connemara fishing village—and sets out to find himself a whore. His drinking companion in the local pub directs him to the house of a woman living alone with her retarded brother in a remote part of the countryside. It transpires that she is the victim of a cruel joke: she is not a prostitute, and has been exiled from the community since her unmarried pregnancy brought misfortune on her family. The sailor feels sorry for her and resolves to return the next day to escort her to Mass in the village. But the priest from whom he hears her story insists she is better off isolated and persuades him to give up his plan. He drinks himself into insensibility and embarks the following day, cursing the Irish.

O'Faolain makes the most of the encounters between the sailor and one Jamesy Dinny John—or as the Frenchman renders it, Jamesy Denijon—in order to inject a note of levity into his rather bleak subject. In fact, it may be said in Jamesy's defense that the sailor's incomprehension of rural Ireland prompts him to invention. Together they banter with the barmaid, but the sailor does not understand that it is no more than banter, and when he attempts to get on more familiar terms with her, she quickly if somewhat mystifyingly puts him in his place:

> "But are you a good girl?" he asked her.
> "I'd be very bad, now, then . . . if I'm not half as good as whoever you left behind where you last drew anchor." (*CS*, 213)

Repulsed as much by her verbal dexterity as by her manner, he falls back upon Jamesy:

> "Jamesy," sighed the sailor, coming to the point. "When a man is on the sea he has no wife."
> "The divil a wife, by Jawsus!" croaked Jamesy at the top of his palate, "but you're better off not to be breaking your melt keeping time with them." (*CS*, 213)

He persists, and Jamesy gets the message at last. "There's no Kitty the Wrens in this part of the world" (*CS*, 214), he insists, but the sailor mistakes the generic term for the name of a particular woman—and Jamesy remembers the unfortunate Kitty, who is the subject of so many stories in the community that, for all he claims to know, she may well answer to the sailor's need.

The sailor cycles 12 miles through desolate bog and rock. When he finally encounters Kitty, she seems a simple unaffected creature, but is quick to undeceive him. He asks permission to rest at her cabin before he begins the long journey back to the village. In a poignant conversation, the isolation of her joyless life is revealed. Her only contact with the outside world is through her retarded brother, whom she sends to the village for food. She is reduced to perusing a schoolgirl's reader for entertainment and regards herself as degraded because she cannot go to Mass. Far from being promiscuous, she solemnly pronounces the original purpose of the sailor's visit "a mortal sin." She examines his earrings with childish awe and is so overcome by his gift of a pair of slippers that the sailor himself is moved. He resolves to return the next day to take her to Mass.

Back in the village, he makes inquiries and pieces together Kitty's story from reluctant informants. "She's sound enough in the head," a storekeeper tells him: "But she got into trouble, thereabout ten years ago. There was a child. One of the lads from around this place it was, as a matter of fact. He ran to America. 'Twas then her father, poor man, went wild. He drank himself into a fury and he was missing for three days. They found the body, God help him, in a bog-hole" (*CS*, 221). The storekeeper concludes that "women like that . . . should be hunted out of the country" (*CS*, 221). Eluded by Jamesy Denijon and somewhat daunted by this vehement misogyny, the sailor wanders by the church and falls into conversation with a friendly parish priest. Again he raises the subject of Kitty Canavan. The priest is concerned to know when his boat leaves and how he proposes to spend his last night in the village. The sailor decides to get drunk instead of bringing Kitty to the village, and the priest bestows his tacit approval. When the sailor voices a final protest that "there is nothing on earth she would like better than to come to Mass," the priest offers the following apology for the behavior of his parishioners: "No doubt. . . . But it's the least part of her punishment. Leave her, my child, . . . to her solitude. It's a lonely glen, but it can be lovely. God, my child, deals with His little creatures in His own way—a more kindly way than our way. Take her from where she is, and . . ."

His eyes roved to the handful of houses that made up Croghan-beag (*CS*, 223). The Frenchman carries out his threat to get drunk. His final judgment upon Ireland is delivered to the captain of his boat: "'*Ny a pas des filles en Irelande. Mais les hommes.* . . . *Ce sont des crevasses, des moules, des* . . .'" (*CS*, 224).

This story presents rural Ireland in the grip of an iron prejudice, steeped in misogyny, incapable of sympathy. Jamesy, at first a comic figure, is revealed as a drunken old busybody who cannot forbear compounding the girl's plight by the grotesque joke of representing her to the sailor as a prostitute. Even the priest is powerless in the face of his narrow-minded community and makes a mockery of his office in his connivance at their inhumanity.

But the story is saved from being merely an angry indictment of intolerance by the fact that it is told from the point of view of an outsider. Our concern is primarily with the sailor; our interest is in his progress from amusement through incomprehension to angry disillusionment. We see through *his* eyes the unfortunate Kitty condemned by her society and thus gain a certain distance from that society—whereas in stories like "A Born Genius" and "Admiring the Scenery" we are virtually constrained to suffer with Lenihan and Hanafan all the bitterness of their inescapable fates. Kitty's saintly demeanor, confirmed by the priest in the rather quantitative terms of the confessional, provides an elegant foil to the sailor's anger, an unspoken reproach to complement his cry of rage. O'Faolain steps back here from the difficulties of life in Ireland and tries to imagine an outsider's view. It is not a pretty picture, but we do not feel the author overreaching himself to tell us so. His Frenchman does that job quite nicely for him, and thus O'Faolain attains for a moment the detachment from his subject that gives his mature stories their power.

O'Faolain is also working to a much greater extent within the conventions of the modern short story, striving for greater compression of characterization and plot, and muting the discursive narrator. He has written that he regards the modern tendency toward compression in the short story as "its peak of technical perfection" (*TSS*, 201–2), and he praises Hemingway's "The Light of the World" as a fine example of this compression. But it is clear he regards Hemingway's method as an extreme, a reduction of storytelling to its most essential elements; O'Faolain may move toward this, seeking an antidote to the excesses of his first stories, but he will never wish to emulate it. His own preference is for a "more suggestive language leaping across deserts of literalness"

(*TSS*, 233), and he will later invent a critical distinction between "Story" and "Tale" to accommodate his need to dilate upon the idiosyncrasies of his characters.

The end of this phrase of O'Faolain's career may be marked by the long ambitious story "There's a Birdie in the Cage," first published separately in 1935 and later included in *A Purse of Coppers*. The story has a tripartite structure and presents three different views of a provincial scandal of embezzlement and dissipation set in the small Irish seaport of Barronloe. As in so many of the stories of *A Purse of Coppers*, its subject is the prejudice and frustration of small-town life, but O'Faolain's attempt to explore the events from a number of different points of view and his deft subjection of setting to considerations of plot and theme set this story apart. It also combines a careful selection of dramatic incidents characteristic of the shorter stories in the collection with a structure that enables O'Faolain to present a more complete picture of his subject than is possible in a story like "Kitty the Wren"; in this, it prefigures his later, more lengthy stories.

The central figure is an Englishwoman, a Mrs. Pomfret, an aging libertine and summer visitor to the town she has had the misfortune to marry into after the death of her first husband. Jim Pomfret, a Catholic, is accused of embezzlement by his Protestant employer and imprisoned, whereupon his wife's social pretensions come to nought. She becomes a sort of pariah, openly scorned for her manners and her pathetic pursuit of the good life. Helen Black, daughter of the man Pomfret has swindled, has fallen in love with Bel, Mrs. Pomfret's son by her first husband. But a deal is struck behind her back by her possessive father and the desperate Mrs. Pomfret. Bel is sent abroad, and the unfortunate Helen feels the cage of Barronloe close about her.

The first chapter presents these entangled relationships from the point of view of Lolly Black, Helen's sister. She takes advantage of Mrs. Pomfret's absence at the trial of her husband to trespass in Pomfret's big house with her young man. Hers is a scornful and envious voice, with a hint of Protestant contempt for a less than exemplary Catholic. She resents Mrs. Pomfret for the excesses of her lifestyle and takes malicious delight in retailing the current rumors about her background: "She really was a nobody. She can be very grand, but sometimes a terrific cockney accent jumps out. I believe it is true she used to dance. He said she was famous at one time and that her name was Violet von Evrement. But I never met anybody who heard of her. Helena says her name was Lizzy Boggs. If she ever danced, it was a long time ago" (*CS*, 304).

Mrs. Pomfret is attached to Helen, but in Lolly's eyes this is no more than nostalgia for her own youth—and a rather prurient nostalgia at that, since she dwells at length upon Helen's physical attractiveness, "looking you up and down with heavy lids, talking of marriage and men, and the way life goes slipping away from you, and the loneliness of Barronloe, and what a lovely body Helen had if she only knew it, and she blowing smoke through her nose at every sigh" (*CS*, 305). The history of Mrs. Pomfret's career in India with her first husband and the disintegration of her first marriage are pitilessly reviewed for the delectation of the boyfriend, who finally puts an end to the tirade by seizing hold of Lolly and kissing her.

Mrs. Pomfret appears to speak for herself in the second chapter, tête-a-tête for the last time with Helen, who is one of her only remaining allies in the town. Lolly's characterization has not been entirely inaccurate. Mrs. Pomfret is beside herself and no longer much concerned with keeping up appearances, as her diction clearly conveys: "Oh, Christ, wot a fool that man was! Wot a bloody fool I was to marry 'im. Oh, don't look at me like that, dearie. I know I didn't ort to use bad language opposite you. You're so good. But it's the bad stuff comin' out. I don't care. I don't care. I must 'ave a good cry. And damn, damn, damn, damn, damn! So there! Think of me what you like" (*CS*, 309). She pines tearfully for her riotous youth in India and curses the bleakness and monotony of Barronloe. Her assessment of herself is not all that different from Lolly's ("I'm a fat, coarse lump of a woman, with false hair and sweaty armpits, and a complexion at two-and-six a jar"), but it transpires that Lolly does not know the worst: Mrs. Pomfret's first husband is not dead. Helen, however, does know, since the distraught woman's son Bel has confided in her. In response to this piece of information, Mrs. Pomfret maliciously discloses that Jim Pomfret, in loco parentis, opposed a match between Bel and Helen because Helen is a Protestant. When she adds that she regarded Helen as too old for her son, the ramifications of the unfortunate girl's plight begin to emerge. Mrs. Pomfret completes her humiliation of the girl by insinuating that her father also had a hand in Bel's departure; what she does not disclose is that Mr. Black bought the separation of the lovers "for twenty-five pounds and the education of her own daughter" (*CS*, 313).

In a powerful and moving third chapter, the abandoned Helen remembers an incident from her relationship with Bel. Together they go boating on a tidal river and are stranded among mudflats by a receding tide. Their relationship is delicately rendered, its nuances all the more poignant in Helen's recollections. She recalls her awareness of Bel's youthfulness and his taunting allusion to her Protestant reserve ("You have their cold look about you"). After futile efforts to escape the mud, they lie down chastely on the boards of the boat and spend the night waiting for the tide. The setting—moonlight, the mudflats, stars twinkling in the pools of water—is a perfect correlative of Helen's predicament, but O'Faolain does not labor the point: "When she awoke they were in the middle of the loch, the sky clouded over, the estuary filled as with milk, and the houses on the far shore watching her" (*CS*, 317). She sees her fate clearly now. She will never see Bel again, and she will die a spinster in Barronloe. Her sister will marry and leave, but she will remain to look after her father. She is trapped in the cage of intolerance others have made for her.

O'Faolain's skillful handling of the dissonant voices saves the story from being a predictable variation on the theme of "A Broken World." The characters of Lolly and Mrs. Pomfret are fully rendered in their speech: the brash, bitchy, envious daughter of a local distillery owner with her petit bourgeois prejudices and aspirations to gentility; the derelict beauty Mrs. Pomfret, bigamist and sybarite, whose vicious and petty nature emerges in her adversity. The only criticism of O'Faolain's method one can make is that he occasionally qualifies the sufficiently informative speeches of his characters with redundant authorial comments, as when he refers to Lolly Black's "pert and youthful hardness" (*CS*, 307) or when in commenting on Helen's final exchange with Mrs. Pomfret he tells us that "the girl had hit on the only piece of truth left in that heavy carcass" (*CS*, 313).

But these are minor reservations. The power of the story lies in the juxtaposition of these two women, unscrupulous in their different ways, with the trusting and sensitive Helen. Here O'Faolain transcends the formula that serves him in so many of the other stories of *A Purse of Coppers*, the eccentric individual trapped by circumstances, whose presence again seems indicated by the title of this story. Helen Black is a victim not merely of life in provincial Ireland, but of her own naïvete—and of a sister and a friend who unhesitatingly place their own interests before hers. O'Faolain generalizes her fate: "She was caught as, sooner or later, all human beings are caught in that coil of things from which there is no escape" (*CS*, 318). Indeed, it is clear her tormentors are no less trapped, Lolly in her studied superficiality and Mrs. Pomfret in the vulgarity she has tried so hard to conceal. Bel alone escapes—but

O'Faolain hints that his time will come. Though fully integrated into the story, the Irish setting is in a sense incidental; betrayal of trust is a universal theme. O'Faolain will never entirely abandon Irish settings, but he has begun to move beyond peculiarly Irish frustrations in search of the universal truth about human relations.

Applied Chekhov

Paul Doyle's study of O'Faolain's work reaches the following conclusion: "O'Faolain's best short stories must earn him the title of the Irish Chekhov."[12] O'Faolain himself has acknowledged the influence of the Russians, saying "the two authors . . . who helped me most would be Chekhov and Turgenev."[13] He does not see himself plowing a lone furrow: he is aware of the example of other writers and freely acknowledges his debt. With Chekhov in particular, he feels a special affinity, and the stories of his second and third collections begin to show the extent to which he absorbs the implications of Chekhov's methods.

In *The Short Story*, O'Faolain illustrates the importance of the personal struggle by looking at the lives of three writers, Daudet, Chekhov, and Maupassant. He finds Daudet at his best in his early stories of Provence; the rest of his career may be regarded as a protracted betrayal of his true subject and self. O'Faolain is thinking here of his own dilemma, of the danger of attenuating his link to his source of inspiration—and of the equally real danger of failing to maintain the necessary distance. Maupassant is not entirely congenial because of his unrelieved pessimism, but he elicits O'Faolain's admiration as a writer who defined his own needs and created a remarkably consistent body of work to satisfy them. Chekhov is a more intelligent writer than either Daudet or Maupassant in that he has a profound knowledge of his own temperament. He is, for O'Faolain, the figure of the successful artist who found his subject in the lives of simple Russians and maintained the delicate balance between bitterness and indifference. O'Faolain does not say so, but it must have occurred to him that his own problem was not dissimilar.

The "concordance between the subject and the temperament of the author" is O'Faolain's preoccupation; the part of *The Short Story* that deals with technique is almost an afterthought. He affects to look dispassionately at three different solutions to the problem, but writes most warmly of Chekhov, and it is clear he is engaged in drawing parallels between his own temperament and that of the Russian. O'Faolain defines the essence of Chekhov as "the frustration that descends on the sentimental mind which deceives itself, which evades reality, and which ultimately breeds lies, smugness, and cant" (*TSS*, 78). Taken as a whole, Chekhov's work is "the affirmation of normality" (*TSS*, 79). But O'Faolain sees this stance is a difficult one to maintain and requires a special type of detachment: "His reserve was immense: he might fuse himself with his people so that what he wrote they spoke: but at the same time . . . he would withdraw himself, as author, from participation in their self-belief. Not otherwise could he be truthful and at the same time natural . . . It is all part of his integrity as a man, which made him so hate sham, and like simple people, and yet not write of the shams without a twinkle or of the simple people without control over his affection" (*TSS*, 81).

O'Faolain admired in Chekhov "the element of belief" (*TSS*, 82), the profound sympathy with human suffering and the fundamentally optimistic outlook reflected in his work. He approves of Chekhov's particular brand of naturalism, which at its best enables Chekhov to hold a middle ground between sentimentality and the souless descriptions of types to be found in Zola. But Chekhov's naturalism is a result not of "matters of craft but matters of faith" (*TSS*, 86). He is interested in the appearances of things only in so far as they present the inner life of his characters:

> No photographs, no absolute externality as of the Naturalists, then, for Chekov [*sic*], and I find it the most admirable thing in him. He did say that he wished only to depict what he saw—but all writers say that, and he saw far more than most. Perhaps it is that he saw in his characters moments as well as men. That was the poet in him. He constantly wrought his people into situations that would satisfy this side of him, situations that opened little windows into their souls where they saw and confessed the mystery of a wider orbit than they or we commonly see, let alone admit, as we go about our daily trivialities. (*TSS*, 93)

Thus, Chekhov, like O'Faolain, is writing about those "moments of awareness" in which we know much more than we ordinarily suspect. O'Faolain finds in Chekhov an echo of his own poetic bent and admires Chekhov's ability to subject the romantic tendency of his descriptions to the demands of a particular story, a skill O'Faolain himself labored to acquire.

Finally, O'Faolain notes that humor and irony enable Chekhov to maintain the role he had assumed, the deeply sympathetic observer of Russian life: "Irony was his one defence against despair. Without it he tended to write out of an abstract disgust. With it he could retain pity and love. A born humorist, too, he always had to laugh at something—smile wanly might be a better word—even if only at himself" (*TSS*, 99). O'Faolain has a more robust sense of humor, and the irony he began to employ in mid-career is perhaps more obtrusive. It is primarily in Chekhov's strategy, his personal struggle, that O'Faolain sees his own journey reflected. He perceives in Chekhov those qualities he has needed and exploited in himself: freedom from provincialism, a fundamentally Christian outlook, independence of all literary or political movements, the emphasis on "normality."

"Lilliput," a story from the *Midsummer Night Madness* collection, is reminiscent of some of Chekhov's early humorous pieces. It relies for its effect on the confrontation between an itinerant mother and her three children and the respectable citizens of Cork. The mother sets up house—a little shack on the back of a cart—in the street, and when a patrol of British soldiers stumbles upon her and her sleeping children, they do not have the heart to arrest her for violation of the curfew. As in a Chekhov story like "Chameleon," the subject matter is slight and anecdotal, and the chief effect is comic. However, O'Faolain substitutes summary for dialogue, to the detriment of this effect. "Lilliput" is unique in being much shorter than the other stories of his first collection—which suggests that its author still needed to write at greater length in order to achieve his ends.

O'Faolain admires Chekhov's "Gooseberries"; he calls it "probably one of the most perfect stories in the whole of the world's literature" (*TSS*, 175). There are some striking similarities between "Gooseberries" and O'Faolain's "Lady Lucifer." In "Gooseberries," two friends, a veterinary surgeon and a schoolmaster, are walking in the countryside, enchanted by nature. Ivan Ivanich, the surgeon, tells his friend Bourkin and the landowner Aliokhin the story of his brother, whose most cherished ambition in life is fulfilled when he comes into possession of an estate on which he can grow and harvest his own gooseberries. The emotion aroused by the story leads Ivan Ivanich to reflect upon the nature of happiness and freedom, much to the dissatisfaction of his listeners. Similar elements are to be found in "Lady Lucifer": the friends' expedition to the countryside, the discussion of an abstract issue (pride), and the example provided by the doctor's story. O'Faolain's evocation of an Irish landscape at once idyllic and soporific parallels Chekhov's perhaps more subtle creation of an atmosphere of longing and frustrated ambition. O'Faolain's "story-within-a-story" is less well integrated than Chekhov's, and in general "Gooseberries" achieves its effects with more economy. But O'Faolain was shortly to begin to emulate Chekhov's technical efficiency.

Both O'Faolain and Chekhov share an interest in the clergy. While O'Faolain does not depict characters with strong and admirable religious faith such as the heroes of Chekhov's "The Student," "The Bishop," and "Easter Eve," he treats his priests and nuns as real and complex human beings. The story "Sinners," from *A Purse of Coppers*, is an attempt to depict the trials of a well-meaning but all-too-human clergy. Frustrated by the worldiness of his parishioners, an elderly canon loses his patience with the halting confession of a orphan servant girl and storms out of the confession box. He's compromised by having listened to the complaints of the girl's employer and oppressed by his inability to control his temper. He takes a walk to calm his nerves and overhears a conversation between the girl and her mistress which brings home to him the duplicity of the girl and the cruelty of the older woman. Turning for home in a renewed state of turmoil, he appeals for God's pity.

There is broad humor in the canon's encounter with the girl. He has already refused her absolution because of her apparent lack of contrition, and she now refuses to admit to any sin at all, in spite of the fact that she hasn't been shriven in five years. The priest prompts her to confess she's stolen her employer's boots, and she immediately perceives he has been forewarned. It transpires she's taken the boots, but not stolen them:

> "Sure I haven't a boot on my foot and she has lashings and leavings of 'em. I was going to put them back."
> "My child, to take them is the same as to steal them."
> "What does she want them for? But she's that mean. Her own daughter ran away from her two years ago and married an Englishman who's half a Freemason. The poor girl told me with her own mouth, only last week, how she's half-starved by that husband of hers and they have no money to have a family. But do you think her mother would give her a penny?" (*CS*, 187)

She reveals she's slept with her boyfriend, but only because she found herself alone in the house during a thunderstorm—"and there wasn't any of that, father" (*CS*, 190). The priest assures her she has sinned, but he fails to impress her with the seriousness of it or to induce in her a penitent demeanor.

The story takes a darker turn when the canon, returning from a late-night walk, passes under the windows of Mrs. Higgins, the girl's employer. He spies Mrs. Higgins, clad in a white nightgown, threatening the unfortunate girl, who has come home late, with the authority of the canon and the nuns. The girl's hatred of her employer is seen to have some grounds. But the girl has lied, insisting that the canon refused her absolution and that she had to wait a half an hour to see another priest. The story closes on this sad tableau: vindictive mistress, unhappy girl, and troubled priest. The priest's state of mind is unsparingly rendered, but with no attempt to present him as the agent of a repressive church; the girl and her mistress are locked in a struggle of their own making. The anger that added a polemical touch to stories like "A Born Genius" and "Kitty the Wren" is absent here; instead of placing the blame on an insensitive and provincial society, O'Faolain has exposed the human motivation of his characters with sympathy and economy. Underneath the humor of the dialogue with the girl, the priest's mounting frustration is skillfully drawn. The composure he attains after leaving the confessional is fragile, and it requires only a snatch of overheard conversation to bring him once again to the pinnacle of vexed emotion.

When this story is compared with others in the same collection, such as "A Born Genius," it is obvious that O'Faolain has gained much in the way of compression and economy of characterization. There is a certain vacillation reminiscent of the early Chekhov in the mood or tone of the story—so that at times we wonder if the author intends us to laugh or cry. In O'Faolain's later stories, this uncertainty is resolved in favor of a broader comedy or an ironic tone imposed by the narrator. "Sinners" differs from a story like "Easter Eve" in that O'Faolain maintains a lively interest in anecdote. He is ultimately more of a story teller than a mood-maker, and though he admires Chekhov's ability to compensate for plotlessness by suggestion and subtlety of associations, he needs to draw the strands of plot more tightly together in his own work.

In a somewhat lighter vein, "Mother Matilda's Book," from the same collection, is a finely written story about an old nun, a former superior of her convent, who is commissioned to write the history of the order. She makes a good start on her project, but age and the deterioration of her faculties overtake her, and the final product is an embarrassment to the convent. The book is exhibited on the occasion of the jubilee of the order, but the nuns conspire to keep the visiting clerical dignitaries away from it, and the story ends with Matilda's disappointment.

Matilda is described thus at the outset:

> In her hey-day, Mother Matilda simply was a goose. She was shapeless as a ball of fur; she clucked and stuttered—her teeth never fitted her—and as the smiling novices hopped about her, she was for ever waving her hands up and down in the air as if she were winging water through the air from the tips of her little fat hands. And as in her youth she had been a goose, in her years she was a wretched little gosling. Her clothes hung from her, she had developed a dropped eyelid, her cowl fell over her blind eye; her voice was a pip-cough. When she slept in the sun, with her breath coming in gusts through her mouth, her face red with sun and sleep, her bibulous coif, and her teeth sinking slowly down to her lower lip, she was a picture nobody in the convent, least of all the novices over whom she once held power, cared to look at. (*CS*, 290)

An outgoing mother superior conceives the history partly in order to keep Matilda out of harm's way. Besides, Matilda is skilled in penmanship. At first, the work goes well, and the unfinished manuscript is borrowed for display by other houses of the order. But Mother Matilda's strength begins to fail her:

> She grew weary of her work. She had copied all the more interesting pieces of illumination and she grew perverse and headstrong and began to invent designs for herself. . . . A little later on she ceased to make capitals, and her round uncial declined into a ragged minuscule, from that into an angular running hand, and lastly into a childish typescript of her own. Because she was too lazy to rule her page it sloped out of the horizontal. There were several errors in spelling and the leaves were often smudged. (*CS*, 294)

The new superior is so appalled at the prospect of exhibiting the ruined book that she places it in an out-of-the-way room in the school building and instructs a novice to make sure that Mother Matilda is also confined to the room. The novice spies a friend from her window and leaves the old nun alone. Matilda makes her way to where the festivities are in progress and renews acquaintance with a jolly priest who attempts to arouse interest in her book. At the critical moment, when the company are about to follow Matilda to view her work, the bishop enters. A shrewd and worldly prelate, he subdues the enthusiasm of his priests and dismisses Matilda with a blessing. The mother superior arrives on the scene, the novice is recalled to her duty, and the unfortunate old nun is returned to captivity with her book. She is finally liberated for supper, but since she has lost her teeth "she could eat nothing, so she spent the whole hour listening vacantly to everyone talking of the excitement of the day" (*CS*, 301).

There is a nice balance between the comedy and pathos of the old nun's plight. O'Faolain describes her infirmities in scrupulous detail, but his keen sense of the comic possibilities of her project prevent the reader from taking her plight too much to heart. This is especially clear in O'Faolain's treatment of the novice who has been assigned to look after Matilda. The novice reflects the impatient attitude of the community in that she hardly seems to regard her charge as a human being. Yet the indifference to age and impatience with infirmity are represented as part of the lot of the pensioner, the nun who has been retired from active duty; Mother Matilda "conspired against" pensioners in her day, and now the younger nuns unthinkingly pay her back in the same coin. Bending over her shoulder, the novice can only look on in horror as the old nun incorporates into her history of the order the "new washer-woman . . . a most praiseworthy and Christian woman," who "has ten children, she tells us, all by different husbands" and is currently married to a "disreputable drunkard of a man." The same juxtaposition of pathos and comedy is found in the interruption of the old nun's efforts to find an audience for her book by the loss of her teeth. Its effect is to distance the reader from the central character, to create a detachment from which her frustration and disappointment can be regarded with equanimity.

The concluding scene of the story enhances this detachment in a particularly skillful way and broadens our perspective still further to include the concerns of the novice and the world outside the walls of the community. Matilda is alone with her novice, grieving that the bishop has not seen her book. Seeing tears in her companion's eyes, she assumes the novice shares her grief. But the younger nun is thinking of her friend, who is ill and may die. As they sit there absorbed in their separate sorrows, they hear the voice of a mother in the slum-alleys outside the walls: "Ja-a-a-anie! . . . Come ho-o-a-me! I'll give you lamb-and-sally when I ca-a-a-atch yeh!" (*CS*, 301).

In *The Short Story*, O'Faolain's refers to Chekhov's characteristic device of effecting a conclusion by merging the circumscribed life of the story with the unseen world that surrounds it. This is what O'Faolain himself does here. The concerns of the individual characters are merged in a suggestive coincidence of disparate events, and the reader is led outward from the dying mind of the old nun to contemplate the isolation of the convent itself and the rude life of the city that surrounds it. In general, O'Faolain has less need of what he calls the "And so it goes on" ending, since his liking for anecdotal plots frequently enables him to tie up loose ends before the concluding lines are reached.

O'Faolain's fondness for depictions of religious life occasionally leads him to give his sympathy a little too readily to characters who are no more than amusing stereotypes. But in the title story of *Teresa and Other Stories* (1947), he shows that he understands the depths of psychology as well as the shallows of religious feeling. Teresa, a young novice uncertain of her vocation, is making a pilgrimage to Liseux in the company of an elderly nun, one Sister Patrick, who intends to visit her aunt, a reverend mother in the Carmelite convent in the town. After various comic misadventures—the girl's wistful worldliness, the old nun's demotic French—the pair reach their destination, attend first Mass, and visit the saint's home. Sister Patrick's aunt is the embodiment of heartless asceticism and the severity of her demeanor frightens the young novice. But at the worldly resort of Saint Malo, Teresa conceives a desire for the mortification of the flesh which embarrasses the old nun. Sister Patrick's comfortable religious emotions (which allow her to indulge a passion for chocolates and to make the most of her vacation) are affronted by what she shrewdly takes to be an affected asceticism. Teresa vows to become a Carmelite, novice and nun fall out—and Teresa's first act on returning to her convent in London is to flee to the home of a married brother and exchange her habit for a tennis frock.

The complex and subtle portrait of Teresa is accomplished largely through a skillful use of dialogue. The young girl kicks against the pricks of the religious life. When she complains of a headache, the old nun tells her to:

> "Offer it up to Saint Teresa for the sake of your intention."
> "I've offered it up on the boat the whole way over," retorted the novice.
> " 'Tis a cross," said the old woman easily. " 'Tis put on you by Saint Teresa to try you. Suffer it for her sake." (*CS*, 322)

This establishes the pattern of their interaction: when one blows hot the other blows cold. When Teresa wonders if her vocation is sincere, Sister

Patrick loses patience and reminds her of the duties of pilgrimage. When the two are locked out of their hostel because Teresa's urgent need of a cup of tea delays them, the old nun threatens to bring a bad report of her to her superior. Of course, Sister Patrick has a heart of gold; she nurses her charge through the crisis of losing her way in the street, and when the forbidding Carmelite aunt confronts the novice with the prospect of life in an enclosed order, Sister Patrick springs to her defense. But when the novice embarks upon a self-imposed regimen of penance, the old nun is appalled and orders her to desist:

> "Sister Patrick," she begged, "I will obey if you command me. But I want to do penance for my sins, and for the sins of the world. I feel I have received a higher command."
>
> "What higher command?" blustered the old woman, taken aback. "What on earth are you talking about, Sister?"
>
> Teresa sighed.
>
> "The sins of the world are all about us," she smiled sadly. "I see them every night from my window, across the water, in the dens and gambling-houses. All lit up like the fires of Hell to lure poor souls astray. I dreamed the first night I came here that the Devil lives over there. I saw his red eyes in the air. I saw that this convent was put here specially to atone for the wickedness that surrounds it."
>
> "Holy Mother!" cried the nun. "What are you talking about, girl? Sister Teresa, let me tell you that if you ate a proper supper . . . And by the same token, Miss, no wonder you have dreams if you sleep on the laths of the bed. Do you," she threatened, "sleep on the laths of the bed?
>
> The novice once more hung her head, and once more she had to be bullied into replying.
>
> "I do, Sister," she confessed unhappily." (*CS*, 332)

The result of this exchange is an uneasy truce, which gives way again to hostilities when the novice announces her decision to join the Carmelites as the pair walk together on the beach before the den of iniquity of Dinard:

> "And what's wrong with our own Order, Sister dear?" asked Patrick of the vacancy before her.
>
> "I feel, dear Sister Patrick," judged the novice, staring ahead of her, "that it is too worldly."
>
> "How is it too worldly?" asked Patrick in a whisper.

"Well, dear Sister Patrick," pronounced the novice, "I see, for example, that you all eat too much." . . .

"I shall tell Mother Mary Mell that you think so," whispered the old nun.

"There is no need, dear Sister. It will be my duty to tell her myself. I will pray for you all when I am in the Carmelites. I love you all. You are all kind and generous. But, dear Sister, I feel that very few nuns really have the right vocation to be nuns." Patrick closed her eyes tightly. The novice continued: "I will surrender myself to the divine Love. The death I desire is the death of Love. The death of the Cross." (*CS*, 334)

There is a lucid understanding of the limits of a worldly vocation like Sister Patrick's—and of the excesses of an affected one like the novice's. The characters are exasperated by each other; Teresa is seeking to dissociate herself from the banality of Sister Patrick's brand of piety, whereas the old nun wants no truck with any religious demonstrations that threaten her comfort. But these issues are never made explicit between them; their conflict turns upon the question of religious commitment, which they use in different ways each as a stick to beat the other. The outcome, thus skillfully prepared for in dialogue, is hardly unexpected: the old woman returns to their community with her charge and retires to her bed weeping tears of rage—and Teresa flies the coop.

In a clever sequel, she returns after two years with a Protestant husband for protection. Sister Patrick declines to welcome her. Teresa shakes her head over her past life, with a nostalgia as superficial as her former asceticism. The last word is given to the somewhat discomfited husband, who is moved to regard his wife as "a very spiritual woman" (*CS*, 336).

O'Faolain's achievement in this story is to see things from a number of different perspectives at once. It is easy to sympathize with the young novice striving to extricate herself from a life of stultifying routine and boredom. But O'Faolain resists the temptation to stack the dice against the religious life. Sister Patrick is an intermittently kindly and innocuous nun whose piety is much less intimidating than that of her Carmelite aunt, and it is no less easy to sympathize with her exasperation in the face of the novice's abrupt mood swings. A final ironic note is sounded in the Protestant husband's sheepish incomprehension. There is no attempt to introduce a moralistic note: the author sets his characters in opposition and withdraws, as from a tableau.

O'Faolain is following Chekhov's example in allowing dialogue and situation to bear the burden of his characterization. We sense the ironic stance of the narrator, but the irony is communicated through suggestion rather than direct statement, as in the concluding line of the story, which points up the husband's incomprehension of his wife's spiritual crisis. In comparing this story with "Sinners," we find a more consistent tone, with less reliance upon plot to bring about a resolution. Teresa's conflict is allowed to work itself out in her reactions to the events of the pilgrimage, and the coda in which she returns to the convent is simply an ironic confirmation of what has already been established by implication.

"Shades of the Prison House," from the same collection, is a minor but technically interesting story. The subject of the story is a prison warder of a rural village, ostracized by the superstitious villagers because he is obliged to guard a condemned murderer and to assist at the hanging. But O'Faolain's focus is on the precocious young daughter of the warder whose isolation in the community is a reflection of her father's. The prejudices of the village are presented through the shrewd eyes of the girl, and the reader is allowed to infer the troubled life of the father.

O'Faolain's opening paragraph is perhaps a little too explicit in that it presents the theme of the story in a nutshell:

> The village kids said that they fell out with Inch Moran because she had "levelled" Padna Calla with a stone. That, as far as they knew, was the truth. They had really outlawed Inch because of the things their fathers and mothers were saying about her father. They had turned against him because he was a warder in the jail; because Bantry the tramp was going to be hanged in a week's time for the murder of Boody Bess; and because they were all terrified of everybody and everything connected with the hanging. (*CS*, 387)

The rest of the story dramatizes this situation, being an account of Inch's adventures on the eve of the hanging. But the narrator provides no more exposition, and the reader must piece together the complexities of Inch's domestic situation from the random events of her day.

Inch begins her day in the company of her two step sisters, who do not speak in complete sentences and are described as mad. But she is a plucky and original child. When the mothers filling their buckets at the pump outside her door ask with unconscious hypocrisy why she doesn't play with the other children, she responds: "I am quite happy where I am, thank you. I have my thoughts to think. They are very interesting thoughts, and very typical" (*CS*, 388).

But Inch, being human, tires of her confinement, and casts around for a way to re-enter the community of her peers. She finds a victim in one Rory Baked Beans, who at any other time would have been beneath her scorn. She seduces him with her knowledge of the mechanics of the birth of puppies and kittens in coal holes and with the promise of an expedition to the top of Pike Hill, "out and out as far as we can go, and look down, and see Nothing! . . . out beyond the wood where they caught Bantry . . . out beyond the quarry where they found Boody Bess" (*CS*, 389–90). The ostensible purpose of this expedition is to regain the admiration and leadership of "the gang," but one can also see in it her desire to escape from the constraint of life in the village and from the half-understood opprobrium that surrounds her father. Rory joins her on the doorstep, heedless of his mother calling him home, and they plan the expedition.

The two mad stepsisters are pressed into the party, and spurred on by Inch the four attain their goal, the summit of Pike Hill. They run across a couple who have come to view the black flag on the tower of the jail through binoculars and to talk about the execution; apparently, the hangman has failed to arrive, and a warder has been asked to perform the hanging. Rory Baked Beans gets bored with Nothing, but Inch refuses to leave. He wanders off alone, the sisters fall asleep, and finally Inch consents to lead them home. The sisters go to their beds "like lambs to the stall." Rory goes to Mrs. Calla's for his supper, and Inch "stood in the dark and kicked stones with her boot toe. Mrs. Calla came out and made her come into her house for her supper" (*CS*, 392). She keeps up a brave front in the face of the adults longing to gossip about the hanging. When asked what she saw on her expedition, she responds: "Nothing. But it was quite interesting, thank you. . . . It was very typical and interesting to all of us" (*CS*, 392).

When she returns to her own house, her father is sleeping by the fire. She smells the whiskey on his breath and goes upstairs to lie in bed with her stepsisters. "At long last she heard him come heavily up the stairs, go to his room, and after a while bed springs creaked. She heard a faint sound of water over the weir, and wondered at it because of the drouth. Then she realized that it was him whimpering in his sleep—like a little dog" (*CS*, 393). Thus the misery of the father's life is lightly touched upon in the last sentences, at its point of intersection with the world of the child. It is the child's world the story presents, a world of concerns

49

inevitably darkened by the father's uncertain position in the village. Apart from the occasional articulation of Inch's motivation, O'Faolain leaves the reader to guess at the effect of her father's position on her. This distinguishes the narrative from his more typical method of development, in which no fact of significance is omitted.

There has been a murder and there is to be a hanging and the villagers have developed an irrational fear of the warder—this much we know. But we do not know how Inch came to have two demented or retarded half sisters or what became of either of the warder's wives, though these circumstances presumably effect his standing in the village. Nor are we told anything specific about Inch's relationship with her father. But we can infer a great deal from the few brief exchanges between Inch and the villagers. She sees through their hypocrisy effortlessly; she recognizes that they are patronizing even in their kindness. Her precocious language reveals a child too familiar with the world of adults for her own good. And the final realization of her father's frailty seems to mark the end of childhood and the beginning of a keener and more painful understanding of the ways of the adult world.

The story is an experiment for O'Faolain in a sort of indirect presentation of events, and while Inch's interactions with Rory and the sisters are not always sufficiently dramatic to compel our interest, we are finally moved by her predicament, by the prison her childhood has become, by the effect of adult thoughtlessness upon a child. "Shades of the Prison House" is reminiscent of some of Chekhov's stories about children. It differs from a story like "A Trifle from Real Life" in that Chekhov makes the child's disillusionment with the world of adults hinge upon a single incident, whereas O'Faolain diffuses this effect throughout Inch's day.

The conceit of "Passion" (from *Teresa and Other Stories*) is a letter from a young man to his lover. In it, he describes a childhood visit to his aunt and her brother in his native Cork. Brother and sister are bachelor and spinster; the brother, one Conny Hourigan, is an avid gardener. While the child and his aunt play cards, some men come to the door to ask Conny to donate his six Easter lilies to the funeral of a pauper child. He refuses indignantly, and his refusal casts a pall over the evening. Both aunt and child reproach him, to no avail. The lilies are destroyed in a rainstorm, and the old man takes to his bed. The writer of the letter understands "that his garden was a sort of torment to him" and wonders if "all passion is an unhappiness" (*CS*, 405). But of course the letter ends with an impassioned plea to the beloved.

Hourigan is the central figure of the story, and in him O'Faolain has created a figure symbolic of human frailty. But the character is completely and vividly actualized through the earthy dialect of his native Cork, his outrage at the request of the lilies thinly masking his guilty conscience:

> "They wanted to blind me that there's none in the shops. I don't believe wan word of it. And if there isn't," his voice kept rising and rising, "why did they come up to *me* for *my* poor little flowers? How fair they wouldn't go down to Bolster has a glasshouse full of 'um? Oh, no! Up to the foola! Me poor little six Easter lilies that I reared, that I looked after as if they were me own children, that I . . . But these buckos have no consideration." (*CS*, 402)

The old man is almost monumental in his defense of what is his, and when his sister murmurs a word of sympathy for the dead, he rises to new heights:

> "That's all very fine, woman, but am I going to give me six Easter lilies because . . . And aren't they me own property? Or aren't they? Amn't I entitled to do what I like with 'um? Or amn't I? . . . And am I going to let a pack of Blarney Lane cafflers tell me up to me puss that there won't be luck nor grace about the house if I don't give me flowers to 'um?" (*CS*, 403)

But the sister is appalled by the curse laid upon the house because Hourigan has "refused the dead" (*CS*, 403). The old man storms out, and when he returns his sister tries to draw him into conversation by reminding him of old acquaintances in the city whom he has outlived. The boy, moved by the thought that "all Cork is out of the wan eggshell," entreats the old man to give the flowers. When Hourigan roars his refusal, his sister can stand it no longer: "No, nor I don't think you'd give them to meself if it was a thing that I was stretched in the next room!" (*CS*, 404).

The merit of this story is in its wise and impartial dissection of human nature. The old man's folly is laid bare, and O'Faolain's humorous use of dialect serves only to emphasize it. It is the fatal attachment we all form to the things we regard as especially ours, the things we appear to hold dearer than life and happiness itself. The old man's selfishness not only poisons his own contentment, but also provokes a nasty response from the mourners, who are determined he shall give the flowers, and punctures the illusion of a close and considerate community the boy would like to cherish. The old man's choice of words is significant, though he is uttering a phrase in popular usage: "these buckos have no consideration" (*CS*, 402). They do not consider that it is no small thing they are asking of Hourigan, no more than he can imagine the pathetic emotions of the child's mourners. Even the aunt is infected by the tide of vexation this simple incident lets loose when she comes to question her brother's affections. The truth of the matter is that everyone in the story, narrator included, is locked in the prison of his or her own feelings, unable to imagine the experience of anyone else.

The presence of the narrator incorporates a dimension of self-consciousness and an attempt to point up a moral. This calls to mind Chekhov's so-called Tolstoyan stories, in which a didactic motive is all too evident. At any rate, the connection between the recollected incident and the narrator's predicament is somewhat arbitrary. The narrator is in the power of his love for his correspondent and thus as deluded as the old man with his flowers, though the recollection of the incident is perhaps a warning, and his conclusion shows him to be capable of detached reflection: "Or is it, dearest one, that all passion is an unhappiness? Are we always looking forward to our joy, or thinking back on it, or so drunk with it that we cannot realize it?" (*CS*, 405). The point is made with sufficient clarity by the story of Hourigan, but it is O'Faolain's choice to draw the narrator into it, both as participant and observer, and in his depiction of the narrator's folly to imply an additional judgment. A comparison of this story with Chekhov's "Gooseberries" shows that O'Faolain has still not mastered the demands of the "story-within-a-story."

O'Faolain again takes the trials of the Irish clergy for his subject in "The Younger Generation," a story from *I Remember! I Remember!* (1962). This story recalls Chekhov's "The Bishop," but O'Faolain's bishop is somewhat more resilient in mind and body and receives a more light-hearted treatment. His lordship is a visitor at the home of a wealthy Catholic family in his own diocese, where he finds himself embroiled in a family dispute and lobbied for his support on all sides. The daughter wishes to marry a Protestant, the mother is hysterical and drinks too much, and the father, Count Toby, is vainly endeavoring to keep the peace. The bishop tries to mediate the Church's uncompromising stance on mixed marriages to the young and headstrong daughter, but in the face of her incomprehension of anything that might stand in the way of her desires, he decides that discretion is the better part of valor and withdraws, leaving the family to settle the affair among themselves.

The meat of the story is a comic interview between the bishop and the daughter of the house. The bishop, not unexpectedly, is a man with little experience of women, who tends towards the traditional, not to say misogynist, view; he deplores the family discord, and while waiting for the maid to bring him an egg flip and musing over a half-written pastoral on his desk he recollects a saying of his gardener, one Philly Cashman: "There's only the wan cure, me lord, for shlow horses and fasht women and that's the shtick!" (*CS*, 587). Instead of the egg flip, he is confronted by the daughter Anne who is handsome in jodhpurs and riding crop and has come to apologize for the behavior of her mother. From Anne's lips, the bishop learns more about her mother than he ever wished to know: the countess has made a "martyr" of Count Toby and is "tight half the day" (*CS*, 589). Nevertheless, his lordship's first stratagem is an appeal to the natural order:

> "It's the most natural thing in the wide world for you to fall in love with this young man, why wouldn't you? When a girl is attracted by the twinkle in a young man's eye, or the cock of his head, or whatever it is that attracts ye in young men"—he invited her smile; she yielded it perfunctorily—"it isn't of his religion she does be thinking. And if a girl does fall in love with a young man, what is more natural than that she should want to marry him? What is more proper, in fact? And, then, Miss Anne, what would be more natural than that I, or any other priest, would want to see that young girl married to the man she loves?" (*CS*, 588)

Of course, the girl is not thrown off her guard by this mixture of platitude and paternalism, and she makes short work of the caveat ("we sometimes have to resist our natural impulses") by pointing out that "mummy . . . wouldn't care if he was a Turk. It's just that . . . she's jealous of me, she always was jealous of me, she hates me, and I hate her, I *do*, I hate her!" (*CS*, 589).

The bishop shifts his ground and presses into service a more down-to-earth analogy. Does the girl belong to a club? The Automobile Club in Dublin? Very good. Are there not rules in this club that, if not observed, can result in your expulsion? Very good. As with secular organizations, so also with the Church of Christ. To which Anne replies: "But there are

rules and rules, there are sensible rules, in England Catholics are allowed
to marry Protestants under dispensation, why should an absolute rule be
laid down here?" (*CS*, 590). The bishop, at a loss, falls back upon the
irrational fact of his authority within his own diocese, and the interview
terminates in a stalemate.

The maid arrives with the egg flip: "Bridie Lynam, my lord" from
"West Cootehill, my lord," (*CS*, 591) which as it happens is the bishop's
boyhood home. He sends her away for sugar for his egg flip, anticipating
"a little gosther about old times" (*CS*, 592). But before the maid comes
back he has to endure the brief apparition of the countess, who complains about the help and hurls herself at his feet, distraught and tearful
("Everybody in this house hates me"), before she is led away by her
apologetic husband. The main returns with the sugar bowl and discloses
that she is leaving the count's employ—to go to England for the sake of
"a boy." The bishop sets aside his interrupted pastoral and writes a letter
to his dead mother, which he then tears into pieces. He completes the
pastoral, but "he felt no joy or pride in it, no more than if this, too, were
a letter not to the living but to the dying and the dead" (*CS*, 593). He
lunches alone with the count and tactfully suggests that he cut short his
visit. The count sadly assents and informs him that Anne is taking a flat
in Dublin. To which the bishop replies: "So she's trying a new club?"
(*CS*, 594).

Though O'Faolain makes the most of the comic possibilities, there is
a barb in his humor. The bishop's predicament is that of his Church, and
his well-meaning platitudes are seen to be utterly ineffective in the face
of the impatience and thoughtlessness of the younger generation. He is
the defender of an institution based on unquestioning acceptance of its
strictures, and the girl effortlessly demolishes his fumbling attempts to
sugar the pill. Not that there is much to be said for the younger generation. Anne is an empty-headed young miss, with little respect for her
elders or for anyone who should happen to stand in her way; the spectacle of
the bishop appealing for her respect for an idea and an institution is both
laughable and pathetic. But there is a man beneath the cloth and the
functions of the office, with his own human needs. He cannot share his
nostalgia for Cootehill with Bridie Lynam, whose sights are set on
England, and he takes what solace he can in a letter to the dead.
O'Faolain gives him the last word, but it is hard to escape the conclusion
that his Church has condescended to speak to the likes of Anne in her
own terms, without material or spiritual gain.

A comparison of O'Faolain's bishop with Chekhov's will serve to point up some of the differences in temperament and style between the two authors. In Chekhov's "The Bishop," an ailing and saintly prelate is visited by his mother and young niece. The visit evokes blissful memories of his boyhood, but he is distressed by the formal and deferential manner with which his mother treats him and by the isolation imposed on him by his office. He is taken ill, his doctor tells him he has typhoid, and he dies. There is neither plot, nor dramatic encounters between the bishop and his family, nor pointed resolution. The story is a detailed presentation of the consciousness of a dying man, clinical in its exactitude, but poetic in mood. To achieve this, Chekhov is at his most self-effacing. Whereas O'Faolain draws humor and irony from the clash between the bishop and the daughter of the house (and makes his broader point about the irrelevance of the Church in the modern world at the same time), Chekhov's bishop simply records his disappointment with his mother's unnatural manner and his deep sense of isolation. We sense O'Faolain's presence, guiding our responses, invoking laughter and pity by turns, ending the story emphatically with the bishop's incautious retort; in Chekhov's story, our attention is held by the events themselves, which pass in random yet intriguing succession as before a camera, until the focus comes to rest on the bishop's vague after life in the mind of his old mother. O'Faolain has told us a good story: he has made us smile and sigh. Chekhov has allowed us to see into the last days of a man's life, in which the inner experience is more important than the external events. At the risk of oversimplification, we can say that O'Faolain's narrative voice, colored as it is by manner of the story teller, places him at a further remove from his subject; even when his subject is the inner life of his characters, he is obliged to present us with the external world of events. Chekhov's gift enables him to create the moods and the movements of consciousness in a seemingly arbitrary but ultimately satisfying form, without intruding the persona of the author or appearing to pull the strings.

In an introduction to a volume of Chekhov's later stories intended to correct the misunderstandings created by what he calls the "scrambled" collections of Constance Garnett and others, Edmund Wilson writes that these stories present "an anatomy of Russian society . . . at the end of the nineteenth century and just before the Revolution of 1905."[14] This picture encompasses the landed gentry, the merchants, the intelligentsia, the bourgeoisie, the clergy, and the peasants. "It is a picture," Wilson writes, "of a feudal society attempting to modernize itself, but still in a state of transition that is considerably less than half-baked" (Wilson, x). Does O'Faolain give us an equally comprehensive picture of Irish life in the twentieth century? While he draws his subjects from many different strata of Irish society, it is important to note that the cataclysmic event had already occurred when he began to write. As the theme story of *A Purse of Coppers* indicates, he was obliged to write about a broken world, and his own involvement in the upheaval of war and revolution made it impossible for him not to choose sides. Thus he lacks the broader sympathy of the Russians he admired, which is a function as much of society as of temperament. Of the predicament of Irish writers of O'Faolain's generation, Maurice Harmon writes: "Yeats had Coole Park and the patronage of Lady Gregory, but revolution had gutted the Big House and left a broken world. The difficulties for the novelist were increased by this breakdown in the structure of Irish society. His Russian models could not solve this particular problem for him; their greatness was in some measure due to their having a hierarchical, traditional, well-defined society."[15]

Thus it is apparent that O'Faolain has found in Chekhov precisely what he needs to conduct his own personal struggle: the antidote to sentimentality or romanticism (to which O'Faolain is given, particularly in the early stories), the reserve or detachment (in O'Faolain's case, the control of his anger), and "the element of belief" (which perhaps came more easily to O'Faolain than the necessary distance—else he would never have risked returning home). In *The Short Story*, one writer takes the measure of another, finds a deep congruity of sympathy, and acknowledges the value of the influence. But their interests and circumstances ultimately diverge. O'Faolain is never quite as much at home in his native land as Chekhov, and when he writes about his own people he adopts their manner of speaking and something of their reserve.

The World in Ireland

In *Teresa and Other Stories* (1947), O'Faolain is to be found steering a middle course between the romanticism of the first collection and the social commentary of the second. His concern is still with Ireland and its people, but he has begun to see in their plight the reflection of a universal condition. This development is now consolidated. The shift from the sober realism of a story like "Admiring the Scenery" toward the lighter, whimsical treatment of character found in "Teresa" is complemented by a search for a deeper more interior meaning in the symbolic possibilities of place and situation, as exemplified in two masterful stories, "The Silence of the Valley" and "Lovers of the Lake." O'Faolain's interest in plot and realistic description of nature persists, but the imposing landscapes of Lough Derg and Gougane Barra are given a broader significance and used to indicate the larger forces of both history and religion.

"The Silence of the Valley," which first appeared in *Teresa and Other Stories*, is set in the remote valley of Gougane Barra in West Cork. Nature is virtually a character in its own right, and the dialogue is juxtaposed with the majestic silence of the countryside. This juxtaposition is established in the opening sentence of the story: "Only in one or two farmhouses about the lake, or in the fishing hotel at its edge . . . does one ever forget the silence of the valley" (*CS*, 358). Four visitors—an American serviceman, a practical Scotswoman, an "incorrigible Celt," and an inspector of schools—are staying at a fishing hotel in the valley, where they are entertained by a jolly, eccentric priest and a singing tinker. The visitors bring the foibles of the modern world into this rural haven; the American wants the hotel run more efficiently, the Scot sings the praises of such "pockets of primitiveness" while enjoying cigars and whiskey in the bar, and the Celt craves some improbable marriage of technology and rural life. They fish and swim in the lake, but their pretentious chatter shows that they have no more than a superficial awareness of their surroundings. It is the priest who first "hears" the silence when he is

57

called away to visit an old woman whose husband, a cobbler and the renowned storyteller of the region, has just died:

> As he sat and looked at the blue smoke curling up against the brown soot of the chimney's maw he became aware, for the first time in his life, of the silence of this moor. . . . Always up to now he had thought of this cottage as a place full of the cobbler's satirical talk, his wife's echoes and contradictions. . . . he frowned as he looked at the fire, a quiet disintegration. . . . He realized that this cottage would be completely silent from now on. Although it was May he had a sudden poignant sensation of autumn, why he could not tell. (*CS*, 364–65)

The cobbler is the representative of a dying tradition of storytelling that has its roots in mythology and draws its inspiration from the land. The priest feels the chill of autumn because he senses the meaning of the cobbler's passing. Later, when he returns to the hotel and cooks eels caught in the lake over an open fire, he gains stature and depth:

> He took off his clerical jacket and put on a green wind-jammer, whose brevity put an equator around his enormous paunch, so that when he stooped over the fire he looked like one of those global toys that one cannot knock over. When the resinous fir-stumps on the great flat hearth flamed up—the only light in the kitchen—he swelled up, shadows and all, like a necromancer. He put an eel down on the stone floor and with his penknife slit it to its tail and gutted it. The offal glistened oilily. While he was cutting the eel its tail had slowly wound about his wrist, and when he tied its nose to a pothook and dangled it over a leaning flame and its oil began to drip and sizzle in the blaze the eel again slowly curved as if in agony. (*CS*, 367– 68)

The visitors laugh at this performance; their sarcasm is contrasted with the demeanor of "four countrymen who lined the settle in the darkness with their caps on and their hands in their pockets . . . perfectly immobile, not speaking, apparently not interested" (*CS*, 368). The priest recalls the cobbler's ribald story about an eel and a pig, and one of the old men wonders "is the cobbler telling that story to Hitler now?" (*CS*, 368). With this phrase, the conviviality of the scene is pierced; the silence of the valley and the mystery of the cobbler's death again make themselves felt.

Throughout the story, silence and mystery repeatedly obtrude upon the affairs of the living. At the wake, the conversation falls into "a trough of silence" when the widow evokes the memory of her husband. While sitting in the sunshine outside the hotel awaiting the arrival of the coffin, the priest reflects that "it is as still . . . as the world before life began" (*CS*, 373). The burial is accomplished against the backdrop of a silence that is "outraged" by the voices of the pall bearers, and when the widow's weeping has ceased and the priest leads the mourners in prayer, they respond "hollowly" (*CS*, 376). The silence that underlies appearances is the burden of the past, the mystery of the unknown, the continuity of the tradition represented by the cobbler and sensed, however imperfectly, by the natives.

But it is the priest who is presented as the inheritor of the tradition by virtue of his superior sensitivity and his awareness of the larger significance of the cobbler's passing. Hopkins[16] and Harmon have pointed out that the priest combines in his person aspects of pagan and Christian traditions. He is likened to a "necromancer" and a "magician," he performs his function in alliance with the old diviner whom the cobbler has instructed to determine the position of his grave, and he is explicitly associated with the eel, a symbol of paganism and a creature sacred to the ancient Irish (Hopkins, 97). The salmon represents wisdom in Irish mythology, and to eat it bestows knowledge and visionary powers; after the burial the priest encourages his companions to feast on it and is thus associated with its particular qualities. Harmon says that the eel is the symbol of Balar or Balor, a Celtic deity who defeated armies by means of an evil eye. The priest is also described as a "porpoise," and of course the fish traditionally symbolizes the Church (Harmon, 102).

The implications of these allusions are complex. The priest has in part assumed the role of storyteller, since he undertakes to retell the cobbler's story about the eel and the pig. But because of his office he has the power to enact the rituals of his Church and thus, unlike the secular storyteller, to serve as a conduit or focus of religious feeling. Is O'Faolain suggesting that the pagan tradition has reached its lowest ebb with the death of the cobbler and that its only chance of survival lies in the institution that supplanted it? The Church in Ireland owes its success at least in part to its willingness to appropriate the rituals of paganism and to adapt them to its own ends—or simply to turn a blind eye to the persistence of customs blatantly pagan in origin. The ribald story of the eel and the pig takes on an added significance if the eel is said to represent the resilience of the pagan tradition and the pig the repeated attempts of the Church to assimilate and subsume its unchristian rituals.

The priest is also the most vital and active character in the story. He summons the visitors to the wake and in the cobbler's house leads the assembly in prayer; the following day he presides over the funeral and burial. When the mourners have dispersed and he is left alone with the visitors, he says, "Why is it, all today and yesterday, I keep on thinking it's the autumn?" (*CS*, 376). The inspector of schools nods sagely, indicating that he too has recognized the significance of the cobbler's passing, while the others display their lack of sensitivity; the serviceman remarks that "In America . . . we call it the Fall," the Celt looks forward to his dinner, and the Scot to "another grand day" (*CS*, 376–77). Thus the tradition of storytelling and the sense of place embodied in the cobbler have given way to modern unrest and indifference. But O'Faolain's conclusion is not entirely pessimistic. The tradition survives in the person of the priest and in the vivid presence of the valley and lake of Gougane Barra. In one sense, the conclusion records a minor victory for tradition over modernism. The optimism of the visitors is clearly seen to be superficial; it is the timeless fatalism of the natives, of the priest and his ally, the dead cobbler, that earns our respect.

Thus we see further evidence of the wise detachment from his material that O'Faolain has attained. The author refuses to take sides in the conflict between rural stability and modern unrest. The moderns bear the brunt of his gentle irony, it is true, but the natives are depicted without undue sentimentality. If O'Faolain mourns the loss of the tradition, he also holds out some hope for its metamorphosis and ultimate survival in the person of the priest. And he gives the last lines of the story to the Scottish girl, who, in spite of her mannishness and liberated views, still places her hope in "pockets of primitiveness" like the cobbler's valley.

Landscape is also a significant element in "The Man Who Invented Sin," which appears in both the Jonathan Cape edition of *Teresa and Other Stories* and the almost identical collection, *The Man Who Invented Sin and Other Stories*, published by Devin-Adair in 1948. Like "The Silence of the Valley," the story is also set in Gougane Barra, at a time when enthusiasm for the Irish language brought many visitors to the Irish-speaking areas of the west. These incursions had a revivifying effect, on both visitors and rural society: "places that were lonely and silent for the rest of the year became full of gaiety during the summer months" (*CS*, 337). The story concerns five such visitors, two monks, two nuns, and a layman who acts as narrator, all boarding together in a small house on the lake. In idyllic surroundings, the nuns and monks become friendly and entertain each other in the evenings with singing and dancing. Though their activities are entirely innocent, the local curate hears a rumor of impropriety and arrives at the house to give them a dressing down. When the narrator meets one of the monks 23 years later, he finds a bitter, mistrustful man who has taken the admonitions of the curate to heart. They bemoan the fact that "nobody wants to learn the language now. The mountains are empty" (*CS*, 347). But the monk does not "approve of young people going out to these places" because—"you know the sort of thing that goes on there" (*CS*, 347). The taint of sin has spoiled the idyll, and the rebuked sinners have retreated to drab lives in the city.

"Lovers of the Lake," which appeared in *The Finest Stories of Sean O'Faolain* (1957), is a superb story about an unfaithful wife who makes a pilgrimage to Lough Derg in order to expiate her guilt. The woman's dilemma seems peculiarly Irish: do her religious scruples, aggravated by the irregularity of her domestic arrangements, demand the repudiation of her lover? O'Faolain's achievement is to make us perceive the universality of the problem. The man, fearing the worst, follows his mistress to Lough Derg and undertakes the pilgrimage himself. The shared experience ultimately unites them, and in its resolution the story transcends the particulars of middle-class Irish society. Two people discover through the unfamiliar experience of pilgrimage that there is another world whose principles and laws are in opposition to the evasions and deceptions, both psychological and social, by which they live.

The couple's relationship is depicted with consummate skill. Jenny presents her decision as a whim: "It's just something I thought up all by myself out of my own clever little head" (*CS*, 459). She represents herself as a typical "good little Catholic girl" who conscientiously performs her Easter and Christmas duties. The pilgrimage is "a thing that everybody wants to do sometime . . . a special sort of Irish thing" (*CS*, 460). Unfortunately she involves the skeptical Bobby in the expedition by asking him to drive her to Lough Derg. He's a pragmatic, self-confident Dublin surgeon; he's not in the least impressed by his mistress's self-deprecation. He informs her shortly that he wouldn't tolerate "any of this nonsense" if Jenny were his wife, and during the journey to Lough Derg he sets himself to wring the truth out of her. She offhands him successfully for most of the way, but it finally emerges that religion is more important to her than she has hitherto admitted or he suspected: "It was never routine. It's the one thing I have to hang on to in an

61

otherwise meaningless existence. No children. A husband I'm not in love with. And I can't marry you" (*CS*, 462). Bobby alternates between pity and exasperation, but Jenny's determination is unwavering, and he is obliged to deposit her at the ferry for the island and to promise to return for her within two days.

Jenny's disillusionment begins with her first glimpse of the island. She had expected "old grey ruins, and old holly trees and rhododendrons down to the water, a place where old monks would live" (*CS*, 464). Instead she sees "tall buildings like modern hotels rising by the island's shore, an octagonal basilica big enough for a city, four or five bare, slated houses, a long shed like a ballroom. There was one tree" (*CS*, 464). As she goes among the pilgrims, checks into the women's hostel, divests herself of shoes and stockings, she feels only "a sense of shame." Kind words from the other pilgrims merely irritate her: "She felt the abasement of the doomed. She was among people who had surrendered all personal identity, all pride. It was like being in a concentration camp" (*CS*, 465). She endures the rituals of the pilgrimage in despair, the circuits of the island in bare feet, the repeated prayers with arms outstretched, the mass devotion in the church. Weak from fasting, she regrets her decision to come to the island, and the heartfelt prayers of the other pilgrims oppress her: "I have no more feeling than a stone!" (*CS*, 466). The best she can manage is the plea of the unregenerate: "O God, please let me out of myself" (*CS*, 467).

Outside in the rain, mumbling prayers that have become meaningless, she confronts an apparition—Bobby. He has concluded that she has come to the island to submit her problem to a higher tribunal: "You feel you ought to get rid of me, but you haven't the guts to do it, so you come up here into the mountains to get your druids to work it by magic" (*CS*, 468). He claims he has come to undertake the pilgrimage in order "to know all about you" (*CS*, 467) and taunts her with her attachment to the comfortable life her husband provides for her. Furious, she brushes past him and resumes her devotions. There follows a masterful description of the rigors of the pilgrimage:

> Exhaustion began to work on her mind. Objects began to disconnect, become isolated each within its own outline—now it was the pulpit, now a statue, now a crucifix. Each object took on the vividness of a hallucination. The crucifix detached itself from the wall and leaned towards her, and for a long while she saw nothing but the heavy pendant body, the staring eyes . . . Bit by bit the incantations drew

her in; sounds came from her mouth; prayers flowed between her and those troubled eyes that fixed hers. She swam into an ecstasy as rare as one of those perfect dances of her youth when she used to swing in a whirl of music, a swirl of bodies, a circling of lights, floated out of her mortal frame, alone in the arms that embraced her. (*CS*, 469)

When she encounters Bobby again, he urges her to understand this experience as the effect of exhaustion and lack of sleep. She angrily rejects this explanation. "The magic working?" he taunts her.

In the morning Jenny is exhausted and calm. She sits outside the women's hostel "like an old blind woman who has nothing in life to wait for but sleep" (*CS*, 471). But when she meets Bobby again, her dilemma is brought before her in all its intensity. He claims to be undertaking the pilgrimage, and his cheerfulness irritates her. She admits to him that his interpretation has been correct: she came to face the reality that she ought to give him up. She reveals she has been wrestling with this decision for the six years of their relationship; her life is a lie because of him, and she longs for the strength to set it right. Bobby tries to make light of it, but it's obvious that he has begun to respect the efficacy of the island's "magic." "He kept staring into her eyes like a man staring down the long perspective of a railway line waiting for the engine to appear" (*CS*, 473).

After sleep, Jenny wakes refreshed. In describing her state of mind, O'Faolain presents to us his conception of the function of pilgrimage in the modern world: "She had received the island's gift: its sense of remoteness from the world, almost a sensation of the world's death. It is the source of the island's kindness. Nobody is just matter, poor to be exploited by rich, weak to be exploited by the strong; in mutual generosity each recognizes the other only as a form of soul; it is a brief, harsh Utopia of equality in nakedness. The bare feet are a symbol of that nakedness unknown in the world they have left" (*CS*, 475).

But lest this seem too much like a profession of faith, O'Faolain balances it nicely with the humane and quietly humorous depiction of human weakness. During the vigil Jenny meets an unfaithful wife, who rejoices in having found "a lamb of a priest" to confess to; a little unprepossessing widower encountered at breakfast presents an uncompromising vision of love ("a divine folly") and scourges himself for not having made his wife happy.

On the journey home, the battle between the lovers begins anew. Bobby refuses to admit whether he has taken the plunge and gone to confession; Jenny mulls over the lessons of her experience and wonders if such renunciation is possible outside the confines of the island: "In the world there might also be escape from the world" (*CS*, 478). They drive west, instead of east to Dublin, and vie with each other to observe the last hours of the fast. They arrive in Galway at midnight, where they return to the world with drinks and a lavish meal and a couple of carefree hours at a dance in a nearby hotel.

Of course, their revelry has served only to postpone the critical decision. They stand for a moment gazing out on a moonlit Galway Bay. Bobby allows that he might do the pilgrimage "properly" the next time and gently invites her to retire. But she insists on preserving what she has taken from the island, at least for one night; they kiss passionately—and retire to separate rooms. Things, we assume, will go on more or less as before, conscience having exacted its small price.

This is a portrait of religious conflict in Ireland. In a way, it is a worldly religion; it does not ask so much. Jenny and Bobby are worldly people; she loves comfort and the status her husband's wealth confers, and is troubled only by the vague awareness of impropriety, by a pitiful desire for some unspecified cataclysm that would "make it all come right"; he is an uncompromising rationalist, unwilling to concede to strange and bizarre experiences, participating in Jenny's world only for fear he will find himself excluded from it. And yet, O'Faolain manages to suggest, there is more to it than that. Jenny's vision of the island as a world apart is real; there is a world of experience that underlies the conventional and the mundane, and it is possible to have access to it, if only at moments. Bobby's reluctant participation in this world has, if nothing else, proved his love for her and made her love him the more. Indeed, O'Faolain hints that the solid foundations of his rationalism have experienced a tremor. As for Jenny, her postponement of love is her token that one can keep the world at arms' length, that if the flesh must exact its due, then so must God. The couple find a temporary peace; their wrangling gives way to a deeper understanding of each other which, O'Faolain asserts unequivocally, has come about through the renunciation the island has required of them.

Maurice Harmon sees "Lovers of the Lake" as a pivotal story in O'Faolain's development. Having created sensitive and intelligent characters like Hanafan and Lenihan who deserved better of their environment—and the comic or pathetic figures I will discuss in the next chapter—O'Faolain eventually comes upon, "a subject that enables him to probe deeply into the question of contradictory forces at work within the Irish character . . . he accepts what he has previously dealt with as comedy and satire but handles it with sympathy and tolerance. Fittingly enough the story marks the climax in form and subject of his long analysis of Irish life in his short stories. Its subtle psychological insight not only transcends his more recent handling of character but also prepares for his maturer and mellower mood in the following collection, *I Remember! I Remember!*" (Harmon, 108).

The Necessary Distance

In certain stories that appeared for the first time in *The Finest Stories of Sean O'Faolain* (1957) and in some of the longer tales of subsequent collections, O'Faolain brings to perfection a technique that allows him to maintain the necessary distance from his material without being obliged to disavow his affection for it. His impatience with the inhibiting effects of Irish society is relieved through the use of comedy and irony, and he avoids the coldness of Joyce's analysis by using the conventions of traditional storytelling. His narrators are completely integrated into their society; they speak its language and understand its foibles. If the comedy at times seems a little too conspiratorial, if the storyteller seems to incline toward the role of spokesman rather than critic, the irony balances this tendency nicely in the best stories and restores the artist's detachment.

Harmon notes that a change has taken place in O'Faolain's conception of his characters. Instead of depicting individuals who struggle in vain with a repressive environment, O'Faolain employs a type of "muddled hero," who "is not particularly aware of social issues and may even be indifferent to the whole question of the natural right to a full development of his potential" (Harmon, 107). It is the character's confusion that allows O'Faolain to treat his subject with more detachment and to exploit the comic potential of the character's predicament.

"Childybawn" is a masterful story of the relationship between a possessive widow and her adult son, whom she has "fastened to her with hoops of comfort" (*CS*, 448). When Mrs. Spillane hears a rumor of her son's impending marriage to a "bold-looking strap" from the bank in which he works, she assumes an air of aggrieved sanctity that induces an ulcer in Benjy and estranges him from his fiancée. Benjy's discovery of his pious mother's weakness for drink and the horses gives him the courage to renew his attentions to his Angela, but the truce declared between mother and son binds them anew—and the wedding is postponed for five years while Benjy waits for her to die.

The opening paragraph shows O'Faolain sketching characters against the backdrop of their milieu with a new efficiency:

When Benjy Spillane's mother got a letter signed "A True Friend" informing her that Benjy had been "carrying on" for years with a young lady in the bank she at once sank beneath all the appropriate maternal emotions. She saw her treasure looted, her future imperiled, her love deceived. She saw her poor, foolish child beguiled, his innocence undermined, his sanity destroyed. At this time Benjy was just turned forty-one, a cheerful man-about-town with a winy face like a Halloween turnip with a candle inside it, a pair of merry bull's eyes, a hint of grey at his temples, and his overcoat hung down straight from his paunch as if he was going to have a baby. He was an accountant at the bank, his rank and his cubicle next to the manager's. (*CS*, 447)

When his mother confronts him, he denies everything and swears his undivided love for her. Not to be deceived, she calls upon the priest and the bank manager, and when these pillars of the community plump for an early marriage, she confronts Benjy with the image of Augustine's repentant devotion to his mother and institutes a scarifying regimen of sanctity and self-denial. Benjy takes a vacation on the continent to restore his nerves, but there is no escape:

The day after he came back from Biarritz he fell down at her feet spouting blood from a burst ulcer, and was rushed off to hospital. Before they started to operate they brought in the priest to him, and by then Benjy was in no state—moral, physical, or strategical—to resist his administrations. It was a close shave; they barely pulled him through; and by the time he was recuperating he was a changed man. The day Mrs Spillane passed a bold-looking strap on the stairs of the nursing home, her eyes as red as her painted lips from crying, and walked in to find Benjy reading *The Life of the Curé d'Ars* of his own free will, she knew that mother love had triumphed at last. (*CS*, 452)

Presumably Benjy has severed his relations with Angela and dedicated himself to celibacy and his mother. The balance of power has shifted to Mrs Spillane; O'Faolain proceeds to shift it deftly back to Benjy. The prodigal, himself on the wagon, discovers that his mother consoles herself with a drop of brandy on the sly. "What a lousy, lonely, empty life I've driven her to" (*CS*, 453), he reflects. He comes upon a few unpaid grocery bills and some betting tickets. He's touched; he buys a bottle of Three Star which he rations out to her, provides her with racing tips, and places her meager bets. But when he visits grocer and butcher and betting office in one afternoon, he forms a clearer conception of his mother's extravagance, and this knowledge gives him the strength to oppose her will. A glimpse of Angela, "the seam of her black nylons as straight and swelling as the line of a yacht" (*CS*, 455), is enough to impel him to his decision. His mother's unholy delight at the news, however, gives him pause. "Go on and get married," she tells him. "And torment some other misfortunate woman. The way you're tormenting me" (*CS*, 456). Their pretenses exploded, they are reconciled over a new bottle of brandy. It remains for Benjy to regain Angela's affection. O'Faolain accomplishes this with admirable economy:

> An hour later, well fortified, he put on his hat and coat and went down to Angela's digs. She was in slacks, and shapely in them, and only that he was not too sure of his ground he would have loved to squeeze the life out of her. Instead she led him into the back parlour, closed the door, walked over to him, and slapped his face. She called him a creeping rat, a cringing worm, a bloody mammy's darling. She asked him did he think she could be picked up and dropped again at his own sweet will. She told him she wouldn't marry him if he was the last man on earth. She asked him did he think she was a common trollop. She asked him why didn't he go and marry his mother since he was so bloody fond of her. To none of this was Benjy in a position to give a truthful, or indeed any, answer. She slapped his face once more. Then she burst into floods of tears on his shoulder. At a quarter to two in the morning the landlady came down in her dressing-gown and threw him out, battered, exhausted, but affianced. (*CS*, 456–57)

There's yet another shift. Their reconciliation has given the mother the upper hand. Benjy remains faithful until her death, keeping Angela waiting for another five years. The narrative voice is that of an insider, on intimate terms with the mores of small-town society. But the humor does not prevent the reader from catching a glimpse of the stifling atmosphere in which priest, bank manager, and gossip-monger hold sway over Benjy's (and Angela's) fate. The plot moves swiftly from crisis to crisis, and dialogue is frequently suppressed in favor of a pithy summation that carries almost as much force, O'Faolain's narrator seems to partake simultaneously of two worlds: the milieu of the provincial storyteller whose concern is with local color and the vision of the serious artist who sees the universal in the particular.

"Lord and Master" is a latter-day saga of conflict between the English gentry and the Irish peasantry, specifically between the lord of the local manor and his tenant, an elderly schoolmaster. At issue is a pond seeping underneath the tenant's cottage, which has its source in an ornamental lake on Lord Carew's property, which derives in turn from the river Villy by way of a channel cut by Carew's ancestors down the middle of the main street of the town of Rathvilly. Although the material has tragic potential, O'Faolain's touch is light and the comedy at times almost too broad. But the choice of the schoolmaster as the focus of the story saves the day, for who better to put this small-town struggle in its historical perspective than a cantankerous old teacher whose sensitivity to the injuries inflicted upon Ireland by her nearest neighbor is still painfully acute? In fact, without imposing upon the reader in the least, O'Faolain contrives to make of the conflict an object lesson in history, while in the end he manages to expose some of the tired old clichés and stereotypes that frequently pass for historical truth in Ireland.

As soon as Master Kennedy traces the dampness in the walls of his cottage back to its source in the arrogance of Lord Carew's ancestors, he resolves to redress the wrongs of history and to mount a campaign to dam the stream that has bisected the town for centuries. He buttonholes the county engineer, one Cornelius Cosgrave, a former pupil, and appeals to him as "one of the first young men in this county to take up arms for the independence of your country" (*CS*, 526). But Cosgrave has modified his view of history since the time of his heroic efforts on behalf of Ireland; he talks about "fate accomplee" and the rights of "certain people," whether Saxon or Gael, under the law.

The matter is deferred to the next county council meeting, and though it excites great controversy in the town and heated words are spoken against the gentry, ultimately almost everyone has some reason not to offend Carew. The locals amuse themselves by exposing each other's interests: the bank clerk handles Carew's considerable account; the town's "cryptosocialist" has a sister who works as a parlormaid in Carewscourt; and the former IRA commandant, now a car dealer, who in the good old days was wont to solve all such problems with "one good stick of dynamite," is restrained by the prospect of an order from Lord Carew for "that new Humber Hawk" (*CS*, 529).

A petition for the preservation of the stream, bearing the signatures of the majority of the town's inhabitants, infuriates Master Kennedy: "My God!" he expostulates. "All we've taught the Carews is how to beat us at our own game" (*CS*, 529). So much for the lessons of history. Kennedy spends three weeks canvassing the members of the council and receives assurances of support from all sides. But centuries of oppression have taught the Irish nothing if not how to dissimulate, and Kennedy's support evaporates at the meeting. As of old, the English are single-minded, and the Irish are at odds with each other. The incorrigible tendency of the council members to reduce his lofty grievance to personal and political squabbling might have maddened a lesser man; O'Faolain himself has not always looked upon these peculiarly Irish foibles with such an indulgent eye. But Kennedy beats a dignified retreat: "At the rear of the room the master rose and walked out so quietly that nobody noticed his going. On his way home he almost admired Carew. Outnumbered four hundred to one he could still keep the rabble under his heels" (*CS*, 531).

The old man has recourse to his lawyer, who speaks a modicum of sense to him: "If somebody tried to take away from you something that you and your people had owned for going on two hundred and fifty years . . . wouldn't you fight that man down to the last brass farthing you possessed?" (*CS*, 532). But in spite of the reflection of his own position contained in this, Kennedy will have none of it. He cannot bring himself to imagine what motivates Carew, as his lawyer urges him, and he takes refuge in history: "Do you know . . . what the Carews did to Rathvilly during the Rebellion of 1798?"(*CS*, 532).

The clergy is all that's needed to complete this parody of the past, and the thought of his dead wife's devotion to the Church sends Kennedy, hat in hand, to the presbytery. To his horror, he finds that the enemy has preceded him: the Carewscourt car is parked at the gate. Throwing discretion and decorum to the winds, he bursts into the monsignor's parlor to find the priest conferring with Lord Carew over an ordinance survey map:

> "I knew it," the old man whispered, glaring from one astonished face to the other. "For forty-five years . . . I've taught in this town, and my poor wife with me. I've served you"—he pointed his trembling stick at the monsignor—"since I was a boy serving Mass at the altar, and now I find you conspiring against me with the gentry!" (*CS*, 534)

He comes to the historically logical conclusion:

> "I hoped to find the Church on my side and on the side of my poor wife. But the Church is against us! As the Church was always against us. Against the Fenians. The men of forty-eight. Parnell. Sinn Fein. In the fight for the Republic . . ." (*CS*, 534).

The excitement is too much for him, and he collapses. Carew drives him home, and to the master's horror, he is invited to Carewscourt for a brandy. He gets his first view of the cause of his trouble, "an oblong sheet of water burning below its low granite coping, fiery in the sun that was sinking between a rosy scallop of clouds" (*CS*, 535). The Carews have planted a row of cypress that are reflected in the water, and there are a pair of tritons with fountains spewing from their mouths. In spite of himself, the old man is moved. At this moment, Carew reveals that the house is to be sold to an order of nuns and the lake to be drained to make way for a sunken garden. The old man, still suspecting an ambush, struggles to take this in, while Carew complains about the cost of maintaining the lake. He brings the master into the house. The rooms are stripped; nothing remains but books: "Mostly Irish books," Carew says. "Family history" (*CS*, 536)—for the Carews are Irish too, as the master begins to see. Carew informs him in his tight-lipped English way that he is ill and hasn't long to live. The master admires the house. Carew drives him back to his cottage. Will the sisters put him out of the cottage? the old man timidly inquires: "Carew lifted an uncertain hand, meshed his gears, drove away" (*CS*, 536).

Thus the comic saga ends with one sobering and undeniable historical fact: the demise of the gentry and the uncertain fate of their dependents. There is irony in the reversion of the estate to the clergy and in the exposure of the old man's suspicions as groundless: who is lord and master here? The power of the gentry, the rise of the Church, the force of personal interest and historical prejudice: these are facts that, in the stories of *A Purse of Coppers* and elsewhere, have aroused O'Faolain's ire. Here he takes them lightly enough. The townspeople are comic figures, mouthing platitudes and personal insults, shrugging their shoulders with amused resignation or assiduously attending to their own interests. Kennedy shames them with the sincerity of his rage, but while he is not exactly a figure of fun, a sobering realization is reserved for him. Carew has been trying to rid himself of the lake, and all the intrigue was generated by the townspeople. At the last, Kennedy bridges the gap between Saxon and Gael and feels the sadness of Carew's farewell to his lake. As he sits at home in his own little cottage—which may not be his for much longer—he thinks that he will miss the pond, and thus his plight becomes the counterpart of Carew's. Richard Bonaccorso[17] finds in Master Kennedy's moment of truth a metaphor for the plight of the Irish writer who discovers that his deepest allegiances—to friends, family, and a particular view of history—have blinded him to an entire world, with the consequent impoverishment of his own life and work.

This is a fate O'Faolain is at great pains to avoid. Here he contrives to have his cake and eat it too. He can invite us to take pleasure in those characteristics of his race—dissimulation, historical prejudice, personal interest—that he himself has lately deplored, while at the same time he allows one character to cross the barrier of class and creed and to experience another's humanity. The solution is personal and subjective—or from the writer's point of view, aesthetic—the nightmare of history notwithstanding.

"One Night in Turin" is part of the collection *I Remember, I Remember!* and partakes in the nostalgia that integrates the stories of this volume. The story concerns an aging bachelor by the name of Hunter (whose name locates him within a sporty Protestant milieu), a self-styled man of the world, lawyer, and proprietor of a modest estate near Cork city, from which he periodically sallies forth to sample the more refined pleasures of Europe, and an Irish country girl who has made good abroad, a former opera singer and widow of an Italian count, lately fallen on hard times and returned to Ireland to tempt fate and fortune. Walter Hunter has conceived a passion for Countess Rinaldi (nee Molly O'Sullivan) after witnessing her memorable performance in *La Sonnambula* while passing through Turin in the wake of an unsatisfactory affair, some 14 years before the action of the story. This occasion leaves an indelible mark, and when he hears the news of Molly's return he resolves to risk all in a belated bid for marital bliss. The story describes the elaboration of his proposal and his disillusionment at the hands of the countess.

But "One Night in Turin" differs from the companion stories of *I Remember, I Remember!* in that Hunter's nostalgia is apparently less than profound. O'Faolain treats his character's aspirations with humorous detachment, exposes him as a pompous and conceited dandy in the eyes of a younger rival—and then subjects him to a lesson that, though bitter enough, enables him to reconstruct the complacent persona of the man of the world from the ruin of the would-be suitor.

The opening chapter of the story consists of a series of leisurely recollections of Molly, brought on by the news of her return which Hunter reads in the Social and Personal column of the *Irish Times*. O'Faolain, obviously delighting in this unhurried mode of development, intersperses Hunter's memories with philosophical reflections that serve to establish his character. In the wake of his brief fling on the slopes of St. Moritz with the horsy Betsy Cotman, who "leaped like a chamois from the snow to the bed, from the bed to the snow, oblivious of the chasms that yawned between her inexhaustible store of hearty Anglo-Saxon good cheer and his Irish sensibilities" (*CS*, 643), Walter experiences a moment of rare detachment, in which he suspects himself of having behaved like a fool. Of course, he is immediately moved to generalize rather pompously: "We drag our ego with us through life, chained to it, in its power, not it in ours. We are free of it, or seem to be free of it, only in rare hours—relaxed by the achievement of climbing a mountain peak, elevated by the wonder of some splendid view, asleep, when slightly drunk, listening to music" (*CS*, 644). But this moment leaves its mark; he decides to break with his former idea of himself, and the vision of Molly O'Sullivan, "a sleepwalking snow maiden wrapped in a canopy of cold light and passionate music" (*CS*, 651), falls upon a receptive sensibility.

His experience seems too precious to share with a mob of backstage admirers, and instead he secretly nourishes it through years of casual encounters with her at the resorts of Europe. She marries a count and retires from the stage. The marriage is childless, and the husband falls ill and comes to Rome to consult a specialist. Hunter meets the grieving countess "at Doney's for a nightcap" and tries to wring a confession of unhappiness from her. Her answers strike him as delightfully evasive. He has a great fear of "unworldly women," by Molly, he decides, is "a true woman of the world out of another age" (*CS*, 653). She writes that her husband has died; he sends his condolences. Her apparition upon the stage in Turin has shown him his life of pleasure in a new light: "After forty, it begins to pall" (*CS*, 648). He will go to Dublin, reveal his secret, and throw himself upon her mercy.

O'Faolain packs all this information into the introduction with a great deal of humorous narration but with little action or dialogue. One has the sense that O'Faolain moves backwards in time from the opening scene because he likes to elaborate in a leisurely retrospective manner. But there is also something of the self-conscious mannerism of the storyteller in his mode of exposition. Come here until I tell you a good one, the writer seems to say, but we will be able to enjoy the denouement all the more if we have taken the time to savor the many nuances of Hunter's character. Some may accuse O'Faolain of being long-winded, but here temperament and the striving for an artistic effect coincide.

The chief irony of the story is that Hunter is as much of a fool as a suitor as he was as a Don Juan. Bowled over by the countessa's beauty—though she's as boisterous as a young girl—he is stampeded into a ridiculous strategy. He has come to Dublin, he tells her, in the hope of enlisting her help in winning the hand of a certain woman—whose biography resembles Molly's in all its essential details. In fact, he cannot quite make up his mind about her. As a girl "behind the counter of Katy O'Sullivan's pub in Coomagara" (*CS*, 645), she had put him in mind of Yeats's phrase, "as ignorant as the dawn"; now she asks him shrewd questions about his estate, while in her next breath she reveals that she has been gauche enough to stay at the Villa d'Este in May. He is disappointed to discover that she plans to dine with a young acquaintance of his, George Boyne, heir to a nearby estate, who has described poor Hunter to his face as "the oldest established bachelor in the whole of County Cork! And, by God . . . *still* eligible" (*CS*, 653). When he discovers that the "package" she's asked him to pick up from the cleaners consists of "two frocks, one costume and an overcoat," he decides that "the woman is completely juvenile" (*CS*, 659). However, he has a cliché ready to hand—"no women in the world are more passionate than the Irish and less erotic" (*CS*, 658)—and he parts from her completely enthralled, impatient for their dinner the following evening, at which he has promised to reveal all, unable to imagine how he will pass the intervening time.

The next chapter spills the beans, being written from Molly's point of view rather than Hunter's. Her judgment upon Hunter is swift and telling: "Dear Walter, always fancying himself the lady-killer. I sometimes wonder is he a homosexual, with all that pomade, and the wavy hair, and the smell of *eau verte*, and the tight waist, and the flower in the buttonhole and the dandy's walking stick" (*CS*, 659). Her recollections of Hunter are scarcely as flattering as his memories of her: "I well remember that first morning I saw him on the Green, with Lil Boylan and Judy Helen. Judy nudged me and said, Here's the college Don Juan, so I put on a great laugh, pretending not to see him at all, doing the innocent girl up from the country" (*CS*, 660)—echoes of a more famous Molly here. She doesn't take the story of his lady love seriously, nor is she impressed by his apologies for life in Cork. It transpires that she is eagerly, not to say desperately, awaiting a call from the same George Boyne that Hunter has glimpsed in the lobby on his way out, from whom she entertains some hope of a proposal of marriage. They are obviously on more intimate terms than she and Hunter: "All I get out of him is compliments, flattery galore, the old Irish plamaus, but always dodging off like a trout just when I think, He's going to ask me now. Like a little fox. Sly. A darling, dear, furry little fox, with a long brush. Giorgio! He's only a boy. If he was an Italian I'd know he was only after the one thing. Dear God, if he is, what must he think of me?" (*CS*, 660). There is also one Aldiberti, who might be expected to call her, but he doesn't know where she is staying. She is contemplating her folly in coming to Ireland at all and planning to beat a hasty retreat when the phone rings. It is Giorgio, and she undertakes to meet him in the foyer—and to tell him all about her "amusing lunch" with Walter Hunter. In short, poor Wally was half-right: the woman is a ninny.

It seems as though the storyteller has thrown away the conclusion, but in this kind of story the how of things is more interesting than the what—and O'Faolain has added a few twists to the plot for good measure. Hunter leaves the countessa's hotel experiencing "that triple pain of emptiness, inertia and frustration which man calls loneliness" (*CS*, 661). He sends her roses (*"Carissima, Red Roses for Thee"*) and passes a desolate evening. The following day is positively painful. He catches a glimpse of Boyne in Davy Byrne's and suspects that he and Molly have given him the slip. He flees the city, walks on Dun Laoghaire pier, and dines alone at the Yacht Club. He envisages her "coming toward him now through the dusk, his phantom, seagull-white, smiling with winged lips" (*CS*, 663)—shades of Stephen Dedalus' epic walk on the not-so-distant Sandymount Strand. But reality obtrudes upon his fantasy of their future life; his plan seems wildly improbable, and he remembers she is dining with George Boyne. He throws it all up and drives home to Cork, where at two in the morning before his darkened house he confronts the appalling prospect of a life without her. He turns his car and drives back to Dublin to meet his fate.

Meanwhile, Molly and Giorgio succeed in clarifying their relations, to their mutual dissatisfaction. Boyne is forced into the admission that his love for her cannot run to marriage; the Boyne estate is bankrupt, and his mother has other plans for him—an American heiress rather than the penniless widow of an Italian count. Molly has no intention of settling for anything less, and Boyne revenges himself by enlightening her about Hunter's intentions. She bids him a motherly farewell in the hotel foyer, but her mind lingers upon Wally Hunter. A marriage to the dandy presents itself to her as "a sensible and interesting and dangerous refuge. So close to George. With his rich American wife?" (*CS*, 669) Perhaps the woman is less of a ninny than we thought.

But when Wally arrives at the hotel in response to an unexpected invitation to lunch, the die is cast. Molly has decided to return immediately to Milan. On the brink, he plays his last card, offering her the splendid moment that he has cherished in secret for 16 years, the experience of her voice in the Turin opera that initiated his circuitous pursuit of her. Once offered, it is forever lost, and Hunter is aghast to realize that it has served only to arm her against him. Molly too counts that night as her finest hour. But Hunter's confession has served only to remind her of the strength and power she bartered away for marriage. "Would you dare look for happiness again?" he pleads desperately. The woman of the world suddenly finds herself, with a power of philosophical reflection not inferior to her suitor's:

> "Walter! Nobody ever finds happiness. We make it, the way people mean when they say, 'Let's make love.' We create it. For all I know we imagine it. We make happiness easily when we are young, because we are full of dreams, and ideals, and visions, and courage. . . . But you know what happens to us. That little flame in us that could burn up the world when we're young—we sell a little bit of it here, and a little bit of it there, until, in the end, we haven't as much of it left in us as would light a cigarette." (*CS*, 673)

The fire of courage, she tells him, has deserted her. She leaves him sitting at the table and rushes off to catch her plane, pausing momentarily in the lobby to scribble a self-congratulatory card to the Honorable George Boyne, informing him of *his* fate.

There follows a brief coda, in which Hunter traverses "his little season of hell" (*CS*, 674). He gets off relatively lightly: a day's drinking, a night's debauchery, a couple of bruises, and the loss of some spare change. O'Faolain sends him back more or less intact to life after Molly. His final reflections befit a man of the world: "Ah well! It wasn't such a bad dream. If only I hadn't tried to make it become real" (*CS*, 675). As the story closes, he is trying to make out that his lot is that of humanity. If a broken life of drunkenness and despair seems an equally plausible ending, nobody could possibly hold that against O'Faolain. It is a good story—and everything is in the telling.

"One Night in Turin" shows O'Faolain adapting the form to his temperament and his concerns. In its careful analysis of emotion and shift of point of view, the story resembles "There's a Birdie in the Cage," which prefigures the nostalgic mood of the collection *I Remember! I Remember!* O'Faolain has managed to assuage the reader's natural impatience for the advance of the plot by offering instead a dissection of the nuances of feeling that compels our interest in spite of being almost static, if not actually backward-moving.

The texture of the prose is dense and allusive, its rhythms strong and slow, capable of incorporating philosophical reflections (tongue-in-cheek and otherwise) without disruption. O'Faolain's descriptive language is neither romantically overblown nor bleakly realist; instead it is infused with the sense of a subjective encounter between character and environment, as when Walter Hunter walks on Dun Laoghaire pier under the spell of his Muse.

> He had always liked the force of that stony white arm curved against the ponderous sea. Dublin smoked faintly to the west, low-lying as an encampment, sharp-edged as a saw, pensive as Sunday. Great pink clouds lay like overblown roses strewn along the bruise-blue horizon. Inch by inch the calm evening began to fade into a dusk the colour of cigarette smoke. . . . The white tower and the glass of the many windowed lantern rose coldly above him. When he looked back he saw a few lighted windows along the front. He barely made out the seagulls circling above the mailboat, blue blobs, but he did not hear their cries. The tall windows of his club were greenly lit. Behind the town the Dublin mountains rolled, empty and opaque, as if he were looking at them through smoked glass. Suddenly a yellow finger of light touched the dusty water of the harbour, moved across it, and then the electric string of lamps along the front and down the pier were lit. He climbed the stone steps up the side of the sea wall and went out through the embrasure. There was the night sea, the cold east wind, the sullen wash and slop of waves, one star. (*CS*, 663)

The irony is much more subtle than in a story like "Childybawn." This is due not only to the more sophisticated narrative voice, of a cosmopolitan rather than provincial milieu, but also to the shifting of the point of view. The romanticism of the earlier stories, while giving ground to this irony, has undergone an interesting metamorphosis. On the one hand, it has become the property of characters like Hunter and as such the subject of some amusement. But it has also contributed to the formation of the character of Molly O'Sullivan and a series of female characters who are just slightly larger than life and strain credibility if we regard them as in the realist mode. Did such a creature as Molly ever walk the earth, from the wilds of Coomagara to the opera houses of Europe? Well, perhaps. Do such charming émigrés preserve unspoiled their blend of Irish ingenuousness and European sophistication? More to the point, are they capable in the heel of the hunt of producing such apparently profound philosophical reflections upon their condition as Molly at her farewell luncheon with Wally Hunter? It may be that O'Faolain is involved in the creation of a myth here. At any rate, it is clear that we must take the Countess Rinaldi with a grain of salt.

In a preface to the collection *The Heat of the Sun* (1966), O'Faolain tells us how he regards the development of his technique. He differentiates between a short story and a tale and describes a tale this way: "Like a small plane . . . [it] is much more free, carries a bit more cargo, roves farther, has time and space for more complex characterization, more changes of mood, more incidents and scenes, even more plot" (*CS*, 887). It is obvious that "One Night in Turin" is to be regarded as a tale: it is a complex analysis of the character of Walter Hunter, seen at a number of different stages of life and through the eyes of his beloved and her paramour, and it encompasses much of the history of the character's life, leading him up to an event that might well have been shattering, but leaves him essentially unchanged. "Childybawn" is more obviously a short story, since the character of Benjy Spillane is hastily though deftly sketched, the action does not encompass the span of a life, and the plot moves so swiftly toward its amusing punch line that O'Faolain does not find it necessary to actualize the crucial encounter between Benjy and his intended.

However, looking back, one finds that O'Faolain has employed this distinction between story and tale from the first. Many of the stories of *A Purse of Coppers* and *Teresa and Other Stories*—"Discord," "Admiring the Scenery," "Teresa," "The Younger Generation," to mention a few—meet O'Faolain's criteria of economy of form and movement. But even in his first collection, *Midsummer Night Madness and Other Stories*, in the title story and in "Fugue," we find adumbrations of the storyteller's leisurely mode of development, the shifting point of view, and the philosophical sensibility that begin to be more consciously employed in stories like "There's a Birdie in the Cage" and finally coalesce in a literary form adequate to the writer's mature needs.

O'Faolain helps us to enforce his distinction between story and tale by designating the opening story of *The Heat of the Sun* as a tale. "In the Bosom of the Country" is the saga of retired English army major's struggle to reconcile himself to Catholicism for the sake of Anna Mohan, a woman he no longer loves. Like "One Night in Turin," it opens with a critical event—the death of Anna's husband—and immediately plunges into the past. The history of the major's relationship with Anna and Ireland is recounted, and when the story returns to the present again it is to focus on a series of humorous encounters between the major and his would-be confessor. At moments, the conclusion seems as predictable as that of "One Night in Turin," but O'Faolain is aware of the requirements of the form, and "In the Bosom of the Country," perhaps even more than the sorrows of Walter Hunter, has a sting in its tail.

When the curtain rises upon the illicit lovers, Frank and Anna, Mrs. Mohan suspects the major's loss of interest and is on the point of confronting him. A phone call from the hospital interrupts the scene to inform her that her husband is dead. Frank is off the hook, for now. He's not a subtle man, but something in her expression of grief—"I've lost my poor husband" (*CS*, 700)—makes him nervous. After the funeral he consults a mutual friend who's in the know and learns that he's expected to "make an honest woman of her" (*CS*, 704). He reconciles himself to this after some self-examination and gallantly proposes: "Now, my darling, before the whole world you can be mine" (*CS*, 705).

But after she accepts him with a maidenly blush, he discovers that his religion is an obstacle to a speedy marriage: "Oh, my darling, it would make all the difference in the world if you were a Catholic" (*CS*, 705). His incomprehension turns to irritation as she patiently explains to him the worldly considerations that motivate her request: the diocese will not tolerate a mixed marriage ("Anyway we never did it in our family"), and the society of the little townland will accept nothing less than conversion as the price of assimilation and a fitting atonement for the duration of their scandalous affair. Of course, Anna will understand if he can't bring himself to convert merely for her sake—unless it's the case that he wants to be shut of her.

In between times, O'Faolain wryly describes the dynamics of this provincial love affair. The major has found himself in Ireland in response to the bequest of a house and probably would not have stayed if he hadn't met Anna. The Irish are too cryptic by half for his plodding English temperament, but Anna finds his stolid pessimism endearing, and he in turn makes his peace with her Irish defects of character, "her temper, her tears, her enthusiasms, her wanting always to be smarter than she was" (*CS*, 703). O'Faolain places particular emphasis on Anna's lack of intelligence; it moves him to draw aside and reflect: "Had she been smarter she would have realized that pessimists are usually kind.

The gay, bubbling over, have no time for the pitiful. Love lives in sealed bottles of regret" (*CS*, 701). But as he explores the predicament in which Anna's ingenuousness has placed the major, we begin to suspect that, as the saying goes, she's not as green as she's cabbage-looking.

The major and the monsignor to whom he applies for instruction discover that they have more in common than either one of them might have anticipated. The priest reveals that he has served as a chaplain with the Royal Inniskillings in World War I, and the two men are immediately furnished with a military vocabulary that can be adapted to matters of Catholic dogma. Keene's discomfort with papal infallibility yields to the monsignor's explication of the need for obedience to authority, in war as in religion: "You revere your Queen. The proud symbol of the power of your Empire. We Catholics revere the Pope. The proud symbol of our Empire" (*CS*, 710). The rash pronouncements of the local curate on the escatological consequences of girls in tight jeans provide another obstacle—which the monsignor, again employing military analogy, surmounts by alluding to the distortion undergone by the colonel's orders en route to the sergeants' mess. A rapport has been established, and both men come to look forward with pleasure to their Thursday night dinners at which the major's ascent toward enlightenment proceeds apace, in the genial afterglow of "a sound port" provided by the monsignor and Keene's diminishing store of 1949 Beaunes-Villages.

They come at last to the sticky question of confession, and the major finds his affable host unbending. He has, he learns, committed not one grave sin, but two, by compounding the offense of adultery with the theft of another man's wife. The priest, of course, has been under no illusion about the origin of Keene's interest in Catholicism. He regards Anna Mohan as less than zealous in the practice of her religion and blames the foreign education she received in England and Switzerland. The major is urged to "clarify" matters with his intended, and this, predictably enough, brings down her wrath upon his head. He cannot bring her to admit to anything bearing the name of sin, and it dawns upon him that her Catholicism is of a different stripe than that which he plans to espouse. Anna has no time for the knotty problems of dogma and flies into a rage when he accuses her of complicating matters by affecting to profess for appearance's sake what she disavows in private. Scornfully, she instructs his English simplicity:

> I make it complicated? It is I who am simple about it—your new
> friends who are tying everything up in knots with their laws, and rules,

and regulations, and definitions, and sub-definitions that nobody can make head or tail of. I was brought up on all that stuff. I know it. You don't. They are at it all the time. So many ounces you may eat during Lent in France, so many in Spain. You can't eat meat on Fridays but it's no harm to eat frogs, and snakes and snails. I suppose you could even eat tripe! How much interest may one businessman draw on his deal. How much may another draw on another. Do you think anybody can really measure things like that? A baby who dies without being baptized must go to some place called Limbo that nobody ever knew what it is or in what corner of creation to put it. All that stuff has nothing to do with religion. How could it? Do you know that Saint Augustine said that all unbaptized children are condemned to suffer in eternal fire? Is *that* religion? (*CS*, 715)

The major hastily assures her that once they are married they will never have to talk of such things again, but his confidence has been shaken and a new doubt planted. The monsignor has dealt effortlessly with "Transubstantiation, Miracles, the Resurrection, Indulgences, Galileo, the Virgin Birth, the Immaculate Conception, Grace, Predestination, the Will, Mixed Marriages . . . [and] Adultery" (*CS*, 716), but the best he can oppose to the specter of Limbo is that "it was originally a rabbinical idea" (*CS*, 717). For an awful moment it looks as though Limbo will prove a stumbling block, but Anna saves the day by consigning the innocents to perdition ("To hell with Limbo!") and accusing the guileless major of employing theology to get out of marrying her. He is a stranger among people he will never understand, though he has thrown in his lot with them. At the end of "three weeks of the blackest misery," he submits.

If the exchanges between the lovers are broad comedy, O'Faolain's treatment of the conversion is restrained. The major finds balm for his troubled soul in the brief ceremony—and afterwards the priest invites him back to his quarters for "a good dollop of malt" (*CS*, 720). O'Faolain's attitude towards religion in Ireland is complex. It has mellowed since his description of the alienated priests of "Discord" and "Sinners" and the harsh indictment of "Kitty Wren" and "The Man Who Invented Sin." The priest as character gains stature in "The Silence of the Valley," where he is presented as a link with tradition and the past, and Jenny's ordeal in "Lovers of the Lake" illustrates that even the laity can approach the mysteries. However, O'Faolain has a fondness for worldly priests, and he is not above exploiting the comic potential of the laity's susceptibility to the sins of the flesh. The monsignor has no scruples about speaking to the convert as one man of the world to another, and Anna Mohan is a marvelous caricature of the type of Catholic that could drive a less sanguine cleric to drink. The world and the flesh must exact their due, O'Faolain lightly suggests.

The marriage duly takes place, and everything turns out to Anna's satisfaction. She and the major assume their place in rural society. But it finally becomes clear to the slow-witted major that his wife does not share his new religious fervor. His old friend and confessor cannot help him with this one, and it becomes a bone of contention between man and wife—until Keene's distress is ended by a small epiphany he undergoes one morning while puttering about in his garden. In essence, he seems to have a vision of the unity of all things, and this breaks the shell of egoism that has separated him from his wife. But when he describes it to the monsignor whom he meets in the street, it is obvious that the experience has been trivialized by his foolish enthusiasm:

> "Monsignor! It was something that could only happen in Lourdes! How right you were! Never force things! Change and expand. Move slowly. Live with your problems. There are no laws for hard cases. Trust and courage solve everything. And, as you say, most of those laws are just so many old-fashioned rabbinical ideas. And the decrees of the Councils all lost! Heaven is a gift. The heart is the center. Carry on. We can only all do our best. God loves us. Not a single cross word for two weeks! Everything absolutely ticketyboo. Monsignor, you should be a cardinal." (*CS*, 724)

The old priest, as it turns out, is closer to being a saint. He has nothing to say to this outburst, and two days later Keene learns of his death.

This brings us to a deft and clever little twist by means of which O'Faolain produces a subtle shift in the orientation of his characters. With the priest's death, the elaborate structure of Kenne's conversion and establishment as a pillar of Irish country society falls to the ground. He trades early morning Mass for the domestic comfort of his fireside, and his wife conceives a desire for a more benign climate. Their unspoken bargain is rather elegantly contrived: he will put aside his irritating enthusiasm for religion if she will extricate him from the confusion of Ireland. They plan to go to Italy. Thus the essential frivolity of the laity unmasks itself, and Ireland is left to the best of its priests, who watch over it with a wan and knowing gaze.

With this infusion of irony, the author steps back from his characters.

He had seemed perhaps a little too involved in their fate, and little too amused by his own contrivance, by the comedy he skillfully milks from the uncomprehending major's predicament. Now he looks to his own detachment. He will congratulate neither the priest nor the new wife for having won their man, nor will he applaud the major for having attained religious feeling only to lose it to expediency. In the end, he shows us the big picture, the parallel lives, the all-too-human failings. And yet if he could be identified with any one of his characters it would certainly be the old priest—who watches the affairs of the world with the sad, shrewd, and dispassionate eye of the artist.

The Demands of Memory

With the publication of *I Remember! I Remember!* in 1962, O'Faolain was at the height of his powers as a writer. He had overcome the disillusionment he felt in the aftermath of the Civil War that threatened to limit his work. He had reconciled himself to the state of modern Ireland by looking at it in a historical perspective and by drawing his inspiration from the native tradition of storytelling. As an Irish writer living in Ireland, he had found a literary stance that enabled him to do justice to the complexity of his feelings about his native land. This is the moment he chooses for what must certainly have been a hazardous undertaking: a painstaking examination of the forms of nostalgia.

The narrative voice is central to this undertaking. Harmon describes it as "comfortingly friendly and open, moving along the surface of the story in a deceptively artless and casual manner . . . it suits the narrator in its unhurried pace, its pausing for small and apparently irrelevant ideas and feelings; essentially it is his conversational manner . . . it brings in the omniscient author under the disguise of the trustworthy voice that deals maturely and tolerantly, in a gentle and wise manner, with its subject . . . There is no trace of the haunted, compulsive manner, the reforming zeal, or the apocalyptic tone" (Harmon, 130–131).

O'Faolain is also more interested in exploring the inner life of his characters than in pitting them against a repressive environment. In a sense, his theme remains the same: he is still primarily concerned with the individual's capability for psychological growth. But whereas in earlier work his characters' conflicts have arisen from their ambiguous position within a narrow, postrevolutionary Irish society, "The restricting factors now are internal and an inescapable part of every man" (Harmon, 131).

Nostalgia and memory are themes common to almost all the stories in *I Remember! I Remember!*—but the return of the past is a mixed blessing. In the title story, the bloodless precision with which a young woman's crippled sister recalls the past threatens her own memories, which have to do with feeling rather than events. The inability of the narrator's father to repair an old farmhouse chair ("The Sugawn Chair") demonstrates that he is cut off from his roots in the countryside; but for the narrator their associations with their rural past seem to rejuvenate his parents, and in confronting the wreck of the chair he participates vicariously in his parents' memories: "As I looked at it I smelled apples, and the musk of Limerick's dust, and the turf-tang from the cottages, and the mallows among the limestone ruins" (*CS*, 561). For these and other characters who look back in longing or regret, the countryside is Eden, childhood a time of vivid unrepeatable experience, and memory the only access to this original source of inspiration and value.

The narrator of "The Sugawn Chair" remembers the sacks of potatoes and apples his mother received every October from the farm where she was born. His parents, like O'Faolain's, are living in a rented apartment in Cork city, but they take delight in these reminders of their rural origins, in having, as his mother puts it, a "back." The narrator's father is inspired by the arrival of the sack to repair an old sugawn chair, a relic of his boyhood on the farm. The straw-roped seat has given way, but the father procures a sack of straw and with the help of two cronies and a half-gallon of porter tries his hand at weaving a straw rope. The activity produces an outpouring of nostalgia from the adults, and the narrator, seated on the kitchen table with a friend, is fascinated by the lore of the farm and the countryside with which his parents display an unexpected familiarity. Mother and father begin to talk about their fantasy of retiring to the countryside, although the narrator with hindsight knows "they had not enough money to buy a window box, let alone a farm of land" (*CS*, 560). Their talk recalls for the child what little he knows of the country:

> I could see the little reedy fields of Limerick that I knew from holidays with my uncle, and the crumbling stone walls of old demesnes with the moss and saffron lichen on them, and the willow sighing softly by the Deel, and I could smell the wet turf rising in the damp air, and, above all, the tall wildflowers of the mallow, at first cabbage-leaved, then pink and coarse, then gossamery, then breaking into cakes that I used to eat—a rank weed that is the mark of ruin in so many Irish villages, and whose profusion and colour is for me that sublime emblem of Limerick's loneliness, loveliness and decay. (*CS*, 560)

The memories of the child are mingled here with the reflections of the adult; the dream of the narrator's parents will never be realized, and the villages of rural Ireland will fall to ruin. Even the repair of the chair proves too much for the father. He and his cronies cannot twist the straw into rope, and after much complaining and not a little embarrassment they abandon their project and their nostalgia: "I knew," the narrator says, "that they were three imposters" (*CS*, 561). Years later, cleaning out the attic after his mother's death, the narrator comes upon the chair. He leaves it standing alone upon the bare floor. It is the pathetic symbol of a discarded past, but the narrator is in an indulgent mood. For him, the chair also represents his parents' youth and the rural source from which they drew their appreciation of life and their humanity.

The past returns to Daniel Cashen ("A Touch of Autumn in the Air") in a mystifying recollection of a boyhood visit to his uncle's farm, where he carries food and mail to the old man at work ditching a meadow and then flirts with his young cousin. The recollection is mystifying because Cashen is "neither sensitive nor intelligent" (*CS*, 578); he is a successful businessman little given to self-scrutiny, and it requires a narrator familiar with Proust to reconstruct and interpret his experience. As relayed by this narrator, Cashen's memory is a vision of pastoral harmony which involves a sense of his own insignificance acutely debilitating for the self-made man:

> As Kitty and he slowly jolted along the rutted track deeper and deeper into this wide, flat river basin of the Barrow, whose hundreds of streams and dykes feed into what, by a gradual addition, becomes a river some twenty miles away, the two men whom they were approaching looked so minute on the level bog, under the vast sky, that Dan got a queer feeling of his own smallness in observing theirs. As he looked back, the white, thatched farmhouse nestling into the earth had never seemed so homely, cosy and comforting (*CS*, 580).

The narrator seems to delight in imagining the exquisite detail in which sensory impressions return to Cashen:

> Ferns crackled at the hub. When he clutched one its fronds were warm but wet. It was the season when webs are flung with a wild energy across chasms. He wiped his face several times. He saw dew drops in a row in mid-air, invisibly supported between frond and frond. A lean swathe of mist, or was it low cloud, floated beneath far hills. Presently they saw behind the two men a pond with a fringe of reeds. Against an outcrop of delicately decayed limestone was a bent

hawthorn in a cloud of ruby berries. . . . The sky was a pale green.
The little shaven meadow was as lemon-bright as fallen ash leaves
before the dew dries on their drifts. (*CS*, 581)

As Cashen returns to the farmhouse with the girl, "they heard high above
the bare arches of the trees the faint honking of the wild geese called
down from the north by the October moon" (*CS*, 583). It is a presenti-
ment of death, as the narrator later reveals, but Cashen attempts to
analyze his experience, to ask why he should have remembered this
apparently insignificant event at this particular time of his life, and the
narrator does not have the heart to allow him to see "that we can never
truly remember anything at all, that we are for a great part of our lives at
the mercy of uncharted currents of the heart" (*CS*, 584). For the narrator,
the key to this experience is "the challenging sight of his own [Cashen's]
littleness on the aqueous plain whose streams barely trickle to the sea"
(*CS*, 585) and the reflection of this sense of insignificance on a busy
unthinking life. The setting of this revelation seems equally important;
in the midst of the tranquil countryside, under the influence of boyish
love for a young girl, Cashen glimpsed something so enduring that
it remained with him throughout the long sleep of his life. He dies
unmarried and acknowledges his debt by dividing "a hundred and fifty
thousand pounds" (*CS*, 585) among his relatives who still live in the
countryside of his boyhood. Harmon describes the indirect way in which
O'Faolain achieves his effects in this story. The images of the river valley
in which the men work and the geese that fly over Cashen and Kitty
suggest the passage of time and the immutability of nature. The incident
of the reading of the letters from the old man's sons is suggestive of the
flight from the land and the incomprehension of those who remain
behind (Harmon, 133). Image and incident contribute to the single
effect of Cashen's final sense of loss.

The narrator of "Love's Young Dream" is prompted by the sight of his
son's awkward adolescence to remember his own initiation into love's
mysteries at the hands of two young girls, a cousin in a little cottage on
the edge of the Curragh and the daughter of his aunt's servant on a farm
near the town of Newbridge. His memories are inextricably bound up
with the great plain of the Curragh:

The Curragh is famous for two things, its racecourse on one side of the
plain and on the other the extended military settlement . . . This

settlement is still known as the Camp . . . Sheltering belts of
stunted firs have now been planted along its entire length to protect it
from the bitter winds blowing down from the mountains, whose slow
drum roll closes the view to the southeast. . . . In winter the Curragh
seems older and wider. The foggy air extends its size by concealing its
boundaries. The grass is amber, as if from the great age of the plain.
For one week that November a sprinkle of snow fell almost every day,
so that all the bottoms were white and the crowns of their slopes were
melted green. At dusk the whole plain seemed to surge against the
glimmering cliffs of the distant Camp and only the lights of a travelling car would then restore the earth to its natural solidity. (*CS*, 606)

Needless to say, the narrator is city-born, and this gives to his excursions
into the countryside a heightened sense of discovery. During one of his
visits to the cottage on the Curragh, he quarrels with his cousin, who
refuses to treat him as a man he longs so impatiently to become. A
high-strung adolescent, he storms out of the cottage:

The night was frosty. Not only the Camp but the whole hollow plain
was an iron dish. But I was not aware of the cold as I walked straight
ahead, as hot with anger as a man might be with alcohol . . . It began
to die in me only as the exhaustion induced by constant stumbling in
the dark, the splendour of the sky, the magnitude of the plain and the
cold night air worked on me to cool my rage and fan my desire.
I lay down under the shelter of a furze clump, between the Camp
lights and the cottage lights. Once I thought I heard the coughing of a
sheep. Then I realized that I was hearing only the wind rattling
through some withered thistles near my feet. The wind, the darkness,
the stars, the lights, the size of the plain dwindled me and isolated me.
My isolation turned all these human and sky-borne lights into my
guides and companions. When my head rolled to the north to the lone
cottage, to the south to the windwashed campfires, and looked
straight up to the stars of the Charioteer, I remember shouting out in
my excitement, without knowing what I meant, "The lights! The
lights!"—as if I wanted some pyrotechnic convulsion in nature to
occur, some flashing voice to speak. Only the wind whispered. Only
the dried thistles coughed. (*CS*, 608–9)

He returns to spend a couple of hours in bed with his cousin, but this
affords him no relief since she turns out to be as inexperienced as he: "I
put on my cap after breakfast . . . and spent the whole day wandering,
blind and lost, about the back roads that lead into the great central

bogland of Ireland, an earth-lake of purple heather, where you might tramp all day and see nothing stir except a snipe rising with a whir or, far away, a sloping pillar of blue peat-smoke from a turf-cutter's fire. Its emptiness suited my sense of lostness. I had no wish to arrive anywhere. I wanted to remain undestined. All I wanted was that my other lost self should come back to me" (*CS*, 611).

He flees from his unfortunate cousin to Noreen, the daughter of his aunt's servant, a knowing young woman who leads him a merry dance. The countryside through which he pursues her is imprinted on his memory:

> I turned down one of those aimless lanes that lead under the railway towards the level bog. I had come there across the Curragh. After the plain, open as a giant lawn, this hollowed lane, deep under trees slung like hammocks from ditch to ditch, gave me a queer feeling of enclosure, secrecy and remoteness. I had been there once before during the summer, also in search of her, and I had then got exactly the same labyrinthine feeling that I was going underground. That summer day the lane had been a pool of tropical heat, a clot of mingled smells from the overgrown ditches teeming thickly with devil's bread, meadowsweet, loosestrife, cow-eyed daisies, greasy buttercups, purple scabious, great rusty stalks of dock, briars hooped like barbed wire, drooping hawks-beard. This winter evening these flowers and weeds were a damp catacomb of shrunken bones. The fallen leaves were squashy. The arms of the trees were darkly shrunken against the lowering sky. Once a bird scrabbled. Otherwise there was not the least sound. It became almost dark where the lane descended under a stone railway bridge before emerging to end at a wooden gate, grey and worm-eaten, leading out to the bog, now so vague in the half-light that all I saw of it clearly was the occasional eye of a pool catching the last gleams from the watery sky. (*CS*, 614)

He has his moment of revelation when he spies Noreen in the arms of "a little buttoned-up lump of a fellow with a coarse cap on his head, peaked upward so that what there was left of salvaged daylight on his little, wizened horse's face made me realize that he could only be a stableman . . . As I stood there, petrified, his fist clutched her yellow mop and slowly dragged her head backward. Her mouth fell open like the red gullet of a cat" (*CS*, 616). This moment appears to him in retrospect as an insight into the nature of passion and the fragility of human society. He recoils from this insight, which he identifies as a turning point in his life:

I had wanted to know what there is to know; to possess life and be its master. The moment I found out that nobody knows, I had exposed myself to myself. I would never do it again. The shame of it was too much to bear. Like everybody else I would pretend for the rest of my life. I would compound; I would invent—poetry, religion, common sense, kindness, good cheer, the sigh, the laugh, the shrug, everything that saves us from having to admit that beauty and goodness exist here only for as long as we create and nourish them by the force of our dreams, that there is nothing outside ourselves apart from our imaginings. (*CS*, 617)

His children still visit the farm, now the property of a second cousin, and the cottage on the Curragh has been torn down to make way for a car park. His children make fun of his recollections of the Curragh of his youth, and he has no desire to return. But he ends with a fierce assertion of the power of his experience: "The only thing that would tempt me there would be to feel and smell the night over the plain. I daren't do it. I would still see the flickering lights. I would hear the wavering sound of a far-off bugle. And I would know that these things that I could neither see nor hear are the only reality" (*CS*, 620). His deepest feelings are bound up with the remembered landscape, and in comparison with the gloomy insight of the adolescent all the rest of the narrator's life seems unreal, a pretense.

In "The Kitchen," from *The Talking Trees and Other Stories* (1970), we seem to encounter the narrator of "The Sugawn Chair." His parents have grown old and died in their apartment in the city, but the narrator finds himself the victim of a recurring dream in which he sees a solitary light in his mother's kitchen and then hears the ironic comment of the landlord's son on the old woman's struggle to protect her territory against the landlord's expansionist ambitions. Reviewing the history of his parents' tenure in this unlovely apartment, the narrator represents them as deracinated peasants, insensitive to the ugliness around them, preoccupied with making ends meet. They acquire a veneer of sophistication and familiarity with city life, but all this falls from them in a moment when they receive a letter from a new landlord:

> They might at that moment have been two peasants from Limerick or Kerry peering timidly through the rain from the door of a thatched hovel at a landlord, or his agent, or some villainous land-grabber driving up their brambled boreen to throw them out on the side of the road to die of cold and starvation. The kitchen suddenly became noisy

with words, phrases and names that, I well knew, they could not have heard since their childhood—evictions, bum baliffs, forcibly entry, covenant, the Land Leaguers, the Whiteboys, Parnell and Captain Boycott, as if the bookmaker downstairs slept with a shotgun by his bed every night and a brace of bloodhounds outside his shop door every day. (*CS*, 1054)

The landlord only wants the use of a room, but a drawn out struggle ensues, and at length the narrator's mother, now a widow and an elderly woman, is brought to bay in her kitchen. Can the landlord's daughter fill a kettle of water from her tap once a day? This quest is reluctantly granted, whereupon she is soon called upon to abandon her kitchen and take up permanent residence in a third floor apartment. The narrator consider this to have been a reasonable request, since the third floor apartment is "as desirable an apartment, by any standards, as thousands of home-hungry Corkonians would have given their ears to possess" (*CS* 1056). But he also knows that the landlord has failed to appreciate what her kitchen meant to the old woman: "That red-tiled kitchen had been my mother's nest and nursery, her fireside where she prayed every morning, her chimney corner where she rested every night, the sanctum sanctorum of all her belongings, a place whose every stain and smell, spiderweb and mousehole, crooked nail and cracked cup made it the ark of the covenant that she had kept through forty years of sweat and struggle for her lost husband and her scattered children. . . . He might as well have said to a queen, 'Give me your throne and I'll leave you the palace.'" (*CS*, 1056–57).

So the old woman resists to the death, and after the funeral the narrator meets the landlord's son in the stripped and sorry-looking kitchen. "So this is what all that was about," the young man chuckles. This disturbs the narrator. He sweeps up the debris of the old woman's life and leaves in a daze, swearing that the past is now behind him and that he will never return. But he returns in dreams to the city of his youth, to see the light in his mother's kitchen and to hear the young man's ironic comment on her struggle to defend it. What *was* it all about?

"It was all about the scratching mole," the narrator concludes. He sees his future in his mother's defense of her territory, since it represents the futile resistance of all life to the encroachments of time and age. Thus he can make no peace with the past because it reminds him of his coming end. This knowledge comes between him and the memory of his mother. He is her staunch supporter in her "land war" with the bootmaker, but "when I switch on the bulb over my head I do it only to banish her, to evict her, to push her out of *my* kitchen, and I often lie back to sleep under its bright light lest I should again hear her whispering to me in the dark" (*CS*, 1060). There is another reason to fear memory. His recurrent dream contains not only the vision of his mother's solitary light which rebukes her sophisticated and dispassionate son, but also the figure of the next generation who will look with the same cold eye on all that the narrator himself holds sacred.

In these stories, O'Faolain acknowledges his debt to the past. He still draws his inspiration from the countryside of Ireland, still feels a longing for the unrepeatable experience of youth. He expresses this by creating a series of backward-looking characters who regard the past with a mixture of fear and longing. O'Faolain himself has never lost touch with the past, and so is not as vulnerable to the ambushes of memory as Daniel Cashen, for example, in "A Touch of Autumn in the Air." But he is not complacent about the detachment he has attained. Like the narrator of "Love's Young Dream," he does not wish to return to the scenes of lost innocence—but like his character he acknowledges a powerful atavistic urge, a deep-seated conviction that our most vivid experience is behind us and that life is indeed a long day's journey into night.

Old Wine, New Bottles

At the end of his career, O'Faolain appears as a writer whose subjects have not changed dramatically, though his interests have broadened and his treatment of his themes has acquired depth. He is still interested primarily in Irish life and its challenges and predicaments. He now looks at Ireland in the context of Europe, and his choice of setting frequently reflects the changes that have taken place in his lifetime: the depopulation of the west of Ireland and the growth of an urban middle class divorced from its rural origins. He has attained an almost philosophical detachment which allows him to find humor in what once appalled and outraged him. Perhaps this is in part a consequence of the separation of artist and public figure; O'Faolain has campaigned ceaselessly for liberal causes, but after *A Purse of Coppers*, nothing of his political convictions and very little personal pleading finds its way into his work. His interest in depicting Irish womanhood persists, and there is a series of fine stories that can be said to constitute a sort of composite portrait. Finally, in spite of having discovered the forms of literary storytelling that best suit his subject and his inclinations, he shows himself still willing to experiment and to regard his own process with a self-conscious and critical eye.

After *I Remember, I Remember!*, O'Faolain seems to have turned his face away from the countryside of his youth, and he looks now to Irish towns and cities, to England and to Europe, for his settings. When the retired school inspector of "Hymeneal," from *The Talking Trees and Other Stories* (1970), uproots his wife from Dublin's North Circular Road and brings her to a renovated cottage in the wilds of west Clare, she is less than charmed by the appearance of the place:

> When she got out of the hired car and stood under her umbrella on the roadside, cold and stiff, she saw a white box in a field, oblong, one-storied, wet-slated with two blank eyes. It was backed by a low wall through whose lacy chinks she saw the sunset. She saw rocks, she saw a dark lough blown into froth by the wind. She could barely discern the limestone-grey uplands that she was to come to know as the elephant's hide of the Barony of Burren. That night, from their

bed, she listened for hours to the rain pattering on the tin roof of the turf-shed.

A couple of days later, during a dry, windy hour, she ventured alone on her first walk. She saw a small village huddled below the corrugated uplands. She followed a slim road. On a low rise she came on a ruined castle with six motionless goats on the tiptop of it, their beards blown by the wind. In the far distance she saw a broom of rain gradually blot out a tiny belfry. She saw two cottages whose smoke streamed sideways like two small ships in a gale vanish under the broom. When she got back to the cottage she went into their bedroom to weep in secret. (*CS*, 917)

Fortunately, the inspector comes to realize his folly and his cruelty and returns his long-suffering wife to the Dublin suburbs where they both belong. Apart from a few excursions to small towns of Kerry and Limerick, where life is almost unbearably circumscribed and provincial, this is the last glimpse O'Faolain affords us of the landscape of the west of Ireland. The settings of the most recent stories are predominantly urban and frequently exert a dispiriting influence on the characters. In "An Inside Outside Complex," from *Foreign Affairs and Other Stories* (1976), a lonely bachelor wanders at dusk through the suburban town of Bray. "As he walks through the side avenues between the sea and the Main Street, past rows of squat bungalows, every garden drooping, cottages with sagging roofs, he is informed by every fanlight, oblong or half-moon, blank as night or distantly lit from the recesses behind each front door, that there is some kind of life asleep or snoozing behind number *51, Saint Anthony's, Liljoe's, Fatima, 59* . . . *The Billows, Swan Lake, 67, Slievemish, Sea View*, names in white paint, numbers in adhesive celluloid. Every one of them gives a chuck to the noose of loneliness about his neck" (*CS*, 1099). The estranged suburban couple in "Marmalade," a previously unpublished story included in *The Collected Stories* (1983), rejuvenate their marriage by means of a series of "clandestine" meetings in the Dublin pub where they first met. They consummate their rapprochement in a spinster aunt's tiny house in Ranelagh, with lithographs of Irish castles on the walls and a portrait of Pope Pius X over the bed (they could perhaps have spent a romantic weekend in the west of Ireland—but the thought doesn't occur to them).

In general, an awareness of the Irish countryside and its power is absent from the later stories. The landscape is that of cities and suburbia, and the characters take what consolation they can within the urban setting, without hankering after a fondly remembered past or a rural way of life that has escaped them. Their concerns are predominantly middle class, at best colored with an awareness of Europe. The mountains of the west are empty.

Having attained the distance he needs, O'Faolain can occasionally allow himself the indulgence of drawing close for a moment to those aspects of Ireland that most offend his sensibilities, of raising his voice once more in a protest he knows will be in vain. He does this in two fine stories of the west of Ireland townland of Coonlahan, "Brainsy" and "Of Sanctity and Whiskey," both part of *The Talking Trees and Other Stories* (1970). But though he takes the opportunity to expose the sterility of life in a religious teaching order and the unrelieved monotony of an Irish country town, the tone of these stories is more reminiscent of "Childybawn" than of "A Born Genius" and the other slightly strident stories of *A Purse of Coppers*. Unlike his characters, O'Faolain has, if not made his peace, at least established a working relationship with his homeland. The confining shapes that life in Ireland can assume hold no terrors for him; he describes them with a light touch, with a sense of sadness mingled with ironic humor.

In "Brainsy," Tom Kennedy comes to Coonlahan at the end of his rope. O'Faolain presents him to us, whole and entire, in a deft humorous sentence: "He looked about forty-five (he was thirty-six); his hair was grey as a badger; his lower eyelids were as pink as a bloodhound's; his trousers gave him legs like an elephant; he walked like a seal; and he had been on the booze for some fifteen years" (*CS*, 1005). He's a teacher by default, having failed at everything else he's tried, and he's come to Coonlahan with great reluctance to accept a position at the Abbatian Brothers College; he is himself a past pupil of the same teaching order. His first sight of Coonlahan confirms his worst expectations, and he does not warm to the place as he comes to know it:

> Where he now lodged was with a young carpenter and his wife in a tiny pink house rising directly from the pavement that ended with the school and the monks' dwelling place. Beyond that the road became grass-edged and the countryside began; though within a month, merely by facing the window of the small front room of his lodgings as he ate his dinner—at half past three every afternoon—watching the rare cart or the rare pedestrian that passed slowly by, it came to him that Coonlahan was a place where the life of the country had neither

beginning nor end. Like any one of the little whitewashed farm-houses on the level bogland that he could see through his window it was just another dot in space and time. . . . No wonder that old bus driver had laughed at him the night he asked for "the hotel"! In a place where there was no railway, no cinema, no library, no bookshop, no dancehall, nothing but a handful of shops and pubs? Where, all through the long autumn nights, he soon found that there was nothing whatever to do—after he had corrected his pupils' homework or prepared his own—but to read, or sit with the carpenter and his wife in the back kitchen playing cards, or listening to voices from Dublin fading and returning on the dying batteries of the radio. (*CS*, 1011–12)

But Kennedy's spirits are lifted when he discovers that there's a boyhood companion of his, now a Brother Regis, teaching at the school. In a rush of nostalgia, Kennedy recalls the "purest, sweetest, loveliest years of his life" (*CS*, 1007), his failed vocation for the priesthood, his philosophical disputes with Brainsy, as his friend was known on account of his intellectual acuity and his willingness to challenge authority, civil or religious. But he receives intimations that all is not well with his friend. Brainsy has not been exiled to beyond without reason; Tom deduces from the circumspect utterances of the superior that Brainsy has had a nervous breakdown. Further investigation reveals that Brainsy is at odds with his fellows in the order: he has been censured for the breadth of his reading and has responded by styling himself "the Savonarola of Coonlahan" and castigating the brothers for the petty transgressions of their monotonous lives.

Intrigued—and desperate for companionship—Kennedy attempts to renew their friendship. Brainsy describes to Tom the experience upon which his life has turned: an encounter with a prudish young colleen on the sands of Brittas Bay. Her uncompromising rejection of his advances drives the would-be sensualist into the arms of the Church—but he soon discovers that he has merely jumped "out of the frying pan into the fire" (*CS*, 1016). His problem is that the drab reality of life in the order does not measure up to the ardor of his vocation; his only consolation is that he is a superb teacher, though not the kind who successfully drills students for examinations. When the superior takes Tom aside and asks him to teach Brainsy's history class, Tom fears that he's about to contribute to Brainsy's decline.

But Brainsy is severely injured in a car accident, and when he comes out of a coma after 66 days, it appears that he's no longer in full possession of his faculties. He denies the existence of the soul and the likelihood of an afterlife—"I went into black darkness. And there was nothing there" (*CS*, 1021)—and does not hesitate to expound upon his experience to the local bishop. This gives the superior the excuse to relegate him to teaching Geography, then to spelling—when Brainsy discovers that Geography contains "anthropology, sociology, the study of environments, economics, human values, history, religion, science" (*CS*, 1022)—and finally, to tending the kitchen garden with a deaf and doddering elderly brother.

Tom visits him in his garden in the final scene of the story. The dialogue is handled with great sensitivity, and O'Faolain steers clear of the trap of sentimentality while clearly conveying the outrage of Tom and the stoical cheerfulness of his friend. Tom urges him to come back to Dublin, where they will resume the friendship of their youth. But Brainsy knows that his conduct within the order will ensure that he will not find a teaching position—and there is nothing else he knows how to do. He is resigned to his garden; his apparent insanity has won him freedom from censure so long as he stays there. Tom regards his friend's fate as a living death; he drowns his own sorrow in drink.

This conclusion is as pessimistic as it can be. "Brainsy" is the story of two failed lives. Tom's youthful idealism has given way to drink and despair, and Brainsy's vocation, inspired by ungratified desire, has led to misunderstanding and mental illness. There is more than a hint that Ireland is to blame—the climate of sexual abstinence, the desolation of Coonlahan, the narrow-minded life of the order, the spurious consolation of alcohol. Kennedy's nostalgia for his lost youth recalls the narrator of "Love's Young Dream." But of course Kennedy lacks the stature of that personage who has made a success of his life and looks back in longing, but with a pragmatic sense of the futility of such feeling. "Brainsy" lacks the ambiguity of "Love's Young Dream" and this is O'Faolain's way of dissociating himself from its pessimism. Kennedy has looked to the priesthood, to Brainsy, and at the last to alcohol for justification of his existence; he is ultimately a victim of his refusal to take responsibility for himself. In spite of his predicament, Brainsy maintains a quiet dignity, a Christian refusal to blame his tormentors. The possibility of the survival of the self, even under the most depressing conditions, is hidden from Kennedy, but not from O'Faolain.

In "Of Sanctity and Whiskey," Luke Regan, a past pupil of a later generation who remembers Brainsy as one of his teachers, returns to the Abbatian Brothers College, now named Saint Killian's, to paint a portrait of the headmaster, Brother Hilary Harty. Regan is a "distinguished Academician" (whose colleagues have mockingly dubbed him Luca Fa Presto because of his speed in executing his portraits), and an alcoholic who has been warned to give it up. He cannot remember Brother Hilary Harty from Adam, and he approaches the assignment with some trepidation, not least because of the prospect of four nights in Coonlahan. But he is in need of his commission. He finds the town little changed, though to his relief it has acquired a hotel. His first meeting with his subject does not jog his memory, but the appearance of Brother Hilary Harty moves him to anticipate "the portrait of his life." His nerves steadied by a night of drinking in the bar of the hotel, he begins work. He patronizes the ignorant and narrow-minded old headmaster as he works, quoting from the Bible to appear less worldly and disillusioned than he is and feigning an interest in the affairs of the school—all the while plotting a masterly portrayal of provincial hypocrisy and religious platitude. He recognizes Harty at last as a merciless grammarian, the scourge of the school, who made Regan's boyhood a misery by adopting him for a pet and bringing down on his head the collective scorn of his fellows. Regan resolves to pay the headmaster back in kind, but the recollection disturbs his nerves and he goes to bed "plastered."

Continuing to pander to Harty's prejudices, he completes the portrait. "Never had he felt such a sense of power, energy, truth to life" (*CS*, 1047). He promises to show it to Harty after he has worked on the background—and embarks on a drinking spree that lasts the entire weekend. Roused by Halligan, a fellow past pupil whom he meets in the bar, he proudly displays the portrait. Halligan is suitably impressed, but his wife, a Protestant concerned about her tenuous position in the town, recognizes the danger constituted by such an unflattering portrayal of the powerful headmaster. She summarily forbids her husband to vote for the portrait in the committee of the Past Pupils Union, and when Regan drinks himself into oblivion, she seizes the opportunity to tear the portrait from its frame and burn it. The unfortunate Regan, unaware of the fate of his masterpiece, is removed from the hotel to the school, where he finds himself under the unctuous care of his adversary. Harty promises to help the painter to master his vice, leaves a glass of whiskey by the bed, and departs. The next morning a lay brother, bearing tea for the patient, finds "the glass dry and the body an empty cell" (*CS*, 1050).

This is apparently the victory of hypocrisy and self-interest over art. Harty is allowed to cherish his delusions, and the Halligans avoid being implicated in a scandal. However, Luke Regan is a somewhat questionable representative of art, as O'Faolain is well aware. In his eagerness to take advantage of Harty for his own ends and his inability to avert personal disaster, he reveals himself to be little better than the small town society of Coonlahan he despises. His epitaph uttered by "some wag in a pub" is a mocking one: "He wasn't much of a painter. And he had no luck. But what a beautiful way to die! In the odour. . . . Of sanctity and whiskey" (*CS*, 1051).

There is no simple opposition of contraries here—art versus society, perception versus prejudice—no simple intimation, as in some of O'Faolain's earlier stories, that Irish society by its very nature invariably stifles all endeavor and sensitivity. O'Faolain has reached an art that eschews simplistic generalizations, that is fully capable of rendering the complexity of the relationship between the individual and his society. Coonlahan and the Hilligans are presented with unsparing realism, and though we see Harty mostly through the painter's eyes we cannot conceive of him as particularly likable. But O'Faolain's gentle humor is always present, and its effect is to prevent any such reaction as outrage or identification with one side or other in the conflict. O'Faolain enjoins us to step back from the characters and to see them not as bloodless products of their society but as human beings in all their complexity.

There is a tradition of strong assertive women in O'Faolain's stories who, unlike many of O'Faolain's early heroes, are capable of taking action and prevailing against unfavorable circumstances. Of the heroines of "Teresa," "Lovers of the Lake," and "One Night in Turin," it may perhaps be more accurate to say that their weakness constitutes their strength. Teresa is a light-headed and callow young novice who oscillates between sentimentality and asceticism: it is her very lack of weight and substance that allows her to escape the extremes of religious emotion and to find herself a man. Jenny, of "Lovers of the Lake," is self-deprecating and evasive, a woman who does not love her husband and cannot enjoy her lover. Yet her scruples involve her in a plucky effort to square things with her God, and under the harsh conditions of the Lough Derg pilgrimage she gains a real insight into the nature of religious feeling. Countess Molly of "One Night in Turin," is a type of the successful émigré who returns to Ireland down on her luck and disposed to settle for creature comforts if she can't have love. She is certainly a frivolous scatterbrain, but she has sense enough to prefer an Italian lover to an Irish sinecure, and she pronounces upon the futility of nostalgia with the authority of a sibyl. Compare these heroines and their relatively benign fates with the broken and dispirited men of "A Born

Genius," "Admiring the Scenery," "Childybawn," "A Touch of Autumn in the Air," and the Coonlahan stories.

This series of fortunate women continues with "The Faithless Wife" and "Foreign Affairs" from *Foreign Affairs and Other Stories* (1976) and with "Marmalade" (1982). "The Faithless Wife" tells of an affair between a French diplomat and the attractive wife of an Irish scissors manufacturer. The setting is Dublin, and the diplomat, while awaiting a transfer to a more congenial cultural climate, receives a sentimental education in the ways of Irish women and ends by falling in love. It is an essentially comic piece of writing, and the comedy derives from the clash of cultures, the Gallic man of the world colliding with the evasive and dissimulating Celt. But it's all a matter of perception, O'Faolain seems to suggest, for by the story's end the roles have been reversed, the Frenchman has proposed a domestic arrangement, and the Irish beauty remains bound by pity to the bedside of an ailing husband she despises.

Seen through the eyes of her French lover, Celia O'Sullivan (nee Murphy) is a somewhat ambiguous figure—at least Ferdinand Louis Jean-Honoré Clichy is damned if he can figure her out. Her repeated reminders that she's a Catholic makes him nervous, and he cannot reconcile this with her willingness to cap his slightly off-color jokes. He knows nothing of Irish women, and he seeks enlightenment in Irish literature, where he finds no women at all, "in his sense of the word" (*CS*, 1065). He consults his diplomatic colleagues. A disillusioned Turk opines that "all Irish hohsewomen are in love with their hohses" (*CS*, 1067), and the Italian ambassador informs him that *"Elles sont d'une chasteté . . . FORMIDABLE!"*

The Frenchman is undaunted; for him, all chastity is relative. He finally confronts his enigmatic Irish lass and accuses her of using religion to hold him at bay. She demurs prettily. *Au contraire.* She does not pray: she merely goes to Mass because she is afraid not to, as a sort of insurance policy against the possible existence of a wrathful God. "Amn't I the weak coward, dürling?" she entreats, throwing herself upon his mercy (*CS*, 1067). Ferdy shrewdly refuses to see weakness here. He understands now why she goes to Mass: it is simply for appearances. He has had an insight into Irish womanhood: "You are all of you realists to your bare backsides" (*CS*, 1068). He accuses her of always knowing precisely what she means and wants and of invariably professing the opposite. She tells him she does not like him "one least little bit at all, at all" (*CS*, 1069). They fall laughing into one another's arms—and thence to bed.

As a lover, Celia is "as simple as a forest fire" (*CS*, 1069), but in spite of her lack of refinement, Ferdy is smitten. Her down-to-earth manner does not dilute his romanticism, but the splendid prospect of the affair is darkened when Celia's husband suffers a stroke. He is confined to a nursing home, and from his bed contrives to make the lovers miserable with a barrage of telephone calls to Celia at all hours of the day and night. Their misery is somewhat alleviated when Ferdy vindictively mutters in the invalid's ear that his wife is in danger of collapsing under the strain of looking after him, after which Ferdy receives his permission to take her out and show her a good time now and then. But the husband refuses to die, and the strain takes its toll. Ferdy wants to get himself moved to "Los Angeles or Reykjavik" (*CS*, 1075), but Celia cannot bear the thought of giving up her boutique on Stephen's Green. Besides, though she hates her husband with a passion, her pity will not allow her to abandon him. Ferdy reminds her bitterly that he once admired her pragmatism. Is the care of an invalid to take precedence over a love that was to last forever? Celia rises to philosophy: "Forever? Dürling, does love know that lovely word? You love me. I know it. I love you. You know it. We will always know it. People die but if you have ever loved them they are never gone. Apples fall from the tree but the tree remembers its blossoms. Marriage is different" (*CS*, 1076). Of course, there is the added complication of her two children. The romantic perceives how the land lies. He had thought himself a man of the world, but this Irish wife has initiated him into her own brand of realism.

The coda records that Ferdy contrives to get himself a consular post in Los Angeles and "consoled his broken heart with a handsome creature named Rosie O'Connor" (*CS*, 1078), having apparently acquired a taste for Celtic charm. He has returned to his first opinion of Celia, which he generalizes to include Irish womanhood at large: "They are awful liars. There isn't a grain of romance in them. And whether as wives or as mistresses they are absolutely faithless" (*CS*, 1078). So what are we to think of Celia and this war of the realisms? O'Faolain himself seems a little unsure, though one suspects that he finds something charming even in her faults. She is a woman who professes a religion she does not believe, devotes herself to the care of a husband she does not love, trades passion for position, and is generally as coarse and silly as she can be. But she gives her sophisticated lover an object lesson in pragmatism and leaves us reassured that she will not pine away and die for love of him in her little boutique on Stephen's Green. Perhaps it is best to remember that we view her through the alternately passionate and exasperated sensibility of her lover and to regard the story as a comedy of manners.

In "A Sweet Colleen," O'Faolain plays a minor variation of this theme, the victim in question being an aging Italian confounded by the ingenuous purity of a young Irish colleen in London. The major of "In the Bosom of the Country" goes through similar emotional contortions in his attempt to comprehend the peculiar attitude toward religion of his Irish mistress. Foreigners are fascinated by us, O'Faolain seems to say, but they will never understand us. In "A Faithless Wife," he also shows us the way we are bound by our perceptions and our cultural prejudices. Celia's and Ferdy's affair, though passionate enough, never allows them to meet on common ground; they remain enclosed within their separate worlds, Ferdy consoling himself with tired clichés about the passage of love, the Celia, faithful to nothing but herself, coldly appraising the creature comforts of her world and finding that they suffice.

Here is O'Faolain's commentary on the male character of "Foreign Affairs":

> A monologuist? That was his form, all right! So infectious that one wants to describe it as port winy, portentous, pompous, pomaded. Any other P's? Patchouli? Well, it is, he was, he is an Edwardian hangover. Nevertheless, give the man his due. If he had not had an unfortunate knack of delivering his monologues with such a hang-jawed pelican smile, an archness perilously close to the music hall leer, wink, nudge, lifted eyebrow, he might have ranked with the best of Dublin's legendary monologuists. He lacked their professional self-assurance. However carefully guffers like Wilde, Shaw, Stephens, Yeats or Gogarty prepared their *dits* they always threw them away, assured that there would be an infielder to catch them, an audience to applaud. With Georgie Freddie you were aware of a touch of insecure self-mockery, as if he were always trying to kick his own backside before somebody else did it for him. (*CS*, 1142)

This is Georgie Freddy Ernie Bertie Atkinson, named for King George the Fifth, graduate first class of Trinity College, Dublin, with a degree in classics, major in the British army during World War II, now facing early retirement at 30, his sole place of diversion the United Services Club on Stephen's Green. Needless to say, he's a confirmed bachelor, frightened of women, his only female friend one Moll Wall, "an Irish-speaking, Dublin-born Jewess" (*CS*, 1149), of unprepossessing (and therefore unthreatening) appearance, who occupies an influential (for a woman) position in the Department of External Affairs. Atkinson likes to break a lance with Moll from time to time, but after 12 months or so of retirement he finds himself short of cash and he comes to her for advice. She offers the ingenious suggestion that he should join the Irish Army, where his British credentials will stand to him. He demurs at what seems a step down, but allows himself to be convinced.

He is thus launched on a brilliant career that takes him from the army to the Department of Defence, to External Affairs and thence to the diplomatic service and a post in the European Economic Community in Brussels. His career is stage-managed by Moll, in the hope that gratitude will eventually fan his wary friendship into something like passion. She hopes in vain, and Georgie is straining at his leash. But then fate delivers him into her arms when his surreptitious affair with his Flamande housekeeper threatens to cause scandal. Moll presents him with his alternatives: he can resign and be sent to a post remote from the center of power, or he can announce that he and Moll have a long-standing engagement. The pursuit ends, and the former major capitulates "in the voice of a small boy saying 'Mummy! May I got to the pictures?'" (*CS*, 1166).

Though the story describes a unique and unusual relationship, it is obvious that O'Faolain's real subject is the struggle between the sexes, and in order to treat this subject he has developed a style that is dense and discursive, full of allusions, both literary and local, tending toward philosophical generalization. As in the description of Atkinson the monologuist, the storyteller has stepped forward to address the reader more directly and confidentially, as one loquacious drinker to another across the beer-stained table of a local pub—and rather in the manner of Atkinson himself. The voice is conversational, and the manner of the telling has taken center stage, almost to the point of usurping the interest of the events themselves. The cat-and-mouse game of Atkinson and Moll is more real in the narrator's commentary upon it than it ever becomes in their dialogue; Atkinson is a type of the Irish talker, with not much more than his résumé to distinguish him from his fellows, and Moll Wall, though not of the true Celtic stock, can take her place with Jenny of "Lovers of the Lake," with the Countess Molly, and with the faithless Celia, as a woman who knows what she wants and goes after it.

O'Faolain's concern seems to be to show how these particular events illustrate larger truths. The narrator can rarely resist the temptation to point to the object lesson. The hostility between Georgie and Moll is defined succinctly at the outset: "He feared her—she was female. She envied him—he was male" (*CS*, 1151). Moll knows why Georgie has never made a pass at her: he's "frightened of women, like all Irishmen"

(*CS*, 1151). She's impatient with him when he tells her she's too honest for External Affairs: "She hooted with laughter, well used to male romantics boasting of their realism. Ireland is full of them" (*CS*, 1151). O'Faolain makes Moll his mouthpiece, and she too, like her sisters in this interesting series, discovers an aptitude for philosophy. "You ought to have stayed in Trinity and become a tutor in Ancient Greek," she tells George just before she extricates him from his difficulties with his housekeeper. "I realize now that what you are is a man so afraid of the lonely, little Irish boy in you that you have grown fold after fold of foreign fat to keep him in. Just as this poor woman may well have had an exuberant Peter Paul Rubens goddess bursting to get out of her skinny body ever since the day she was born. O dear! I sometimes wonder how many Ariels were imprisoned in Caliban. And how many Calibans were imprisoned in Ariel? It is a thought that makes one feel sorry for the whole human race" (*CS*, 1165).

Indeed, it is a rather melancholy view of relations between the sexes that O'Faolain presents, in spite of the humor. Atkinson is a little boy, and Moll wants him less as a husband than as a son, a creature of her own making whose success compensates her for the futility of her sex. Irishmen fear women and will do anything to avoid confrontation; in O'Faolain's universe, they are incorrigibly passive and dependent. Their women despise them and treat them as they deserve, thus confirming them in their passivity.

"Marmalade" plays another variation on this theme. It is the story of a couple whose marriage has been reduced to breakfast table trivia. Foley is a spoiled priest who cannot recapture the excitement of a courtship conducted from the seminary, and his wife is a secretary in the Irish Sweepstake who meets on Monday nights to commiserate with a group of women friends equally estranged from their men folk. It's not clear just what Foley's problem is; all we know is that he has refused to make love to his wife on the eve of Good Friday. She accuses him of still being a priest at heart, and when he reproaches her with her own pietistic rituals, she responds "with the passionate observation that God's world is one—joy and pain, crocuses and the crucifixion, love and lust, desire and denial, human passion and prayer" (*CS*, 1234).

When they meet by chance in the pub where he first laid eyes on her as a nervous seminarian gulping a surreptitious pint and casting a cold eye on "life," she encourages his fantasy of having rediscovered the girl he lost in marriage, and their clandestine meetings culminate in a passionate encounter in the bedroom of her aunt's house in Ranelagh, where their courtship was first consummated and the fate of his vocation sealed. But the next morning at the breakfast table, poor Foley is back to square one. He cannot reconcile the woman who loved him in spite of his vow of celibacy with the sphinx across the table who asks primly for the marmalade. He remembers the pronouncement of his parish priest upon his break for freedom: "Once a celibate . . ." (*CS*, 1243). On that glum note, the story ends.

Ellie is a philosopher too. In the course of the couple's weekly dialogues, she makes the following observation: "I happen to see the world as a complex of things beyond all understanding, far too bewildering to be confined or defined by human laws or rules, shall and shall nots. I look at it all as a miracle and a mystery, a place of beauty and horror, a spring flower, a tree in bud, a dead child, a husband dying of cancer . . . a lottery like the Irish Sweep, chance, fate, the gods, God, the Madonna, love, lust, passion, a baby at the breast. Everything is one thing" (*CS*, 1239). By implication, poor Foley is neither fish nor flesh; he has put away the trappings of priestly office, but he still continues to search painstakingly for moral guidance in the domain of fact and reason.

This is heady stuff for a secretary in the Sweep. It becomes apparent that we are dealing with a fiction both more and less than realistic. O'Faolain's characters are not without history or personal idiosyncrasies, but their individuality is increasingly submerged in the national and gender types they are meant to embody. On the other hand, they tend to become mere mouthpieces for the ideas that preoccupy their creator, and these ideas, instead of remaining implicit in the fictional situation (as in a story like "The Silence of the Valley"), are given direct expression and become part of the plot. This gives to many of the later stories a philosophical tone, drawing attention to the narrative voice and away from the characters, with a consequent loss of dramatic tension. It also becomes tempting to reduce the stories to generalizations much less interesting in themselves than either the narrator or his characters. Is O'Faolain trying to communicate his view that women are the passionate realists who accept life and its disillusionments, whereas men are the abstract dreamers powerless to change it or themselves—or in the Irish context that women are hard-headed and unscrupulous, men vein and ineffectual? Does it matter? Against the backdrop of the panoramic fictional world O'Faolain has created in the course of his lengthy career, all such reductions must finally be unsatisfactory.

In "An Inside Outside Complex" from *Foreign Affairs*, O'Faolain conducts some experiments with mirrors. The characters are familiar to us by now: the lonely ineffectual male, imprisoned by the memory of his deceased mother; the strong inscrutable female, who tolerates him as a suitor but without affection. O'Faolain gives a twist to a favorite theme by finding a new way to describe the hero's problem. He has an inside outside complex: when he's outside he wants to be inside—and vice versa. The heroine never looks more attractive to him than on his first glimpse of her through an uncurtained window from a dark and empty street. When he has wooed and wed her and invaded her life, he wants nothing more than to be the sole occupant of one of the other bungalows he sees from the window of her living room. The way out of this difficulty appears when a mirror that does not fit through the door is placed in the garden, and the malcontent can look out at himself looking in. If this resolution seems rather too schematic—all the charm of the story is in the telling.

It begins in laconic storytelling manner: "So then, a dusky Sunday afternoon in Bray at a quarter to five o'clock, lighting up time at five fifteen, November 1st, All Souls' Eve, dedicated to the suffering souls in Purgatory, Bertie Bolger, bachelor, aged forty-one or so, tubby, ruddy, greying, well-known as a dealer in antiques, less well-known as a conflator thereof, walking briskly along the seafront, head up to the damp breezes, turns smartly into the lounge of the Imperial Hotel for a hot toddy, singing in a soldierly basso 'my breast expanding to the ball' " (*CS*, 1098). There is a provisional quality to the prose. A tentative present tense alternates with the more definite assertions of past, and the author seems to be saying to us, here is a possible scenario, if you please—and if you don't like it I can easily change it. Tentativeness is the hallmark of Bertie's nature, outside of his profession, which is dedicated to transforming the inauthentic into the passable imitation. It transpires that it is the anniversary of his mother's death and he has forgotten to have Mass said for the repose of her soul. His life is desolate, especially on weekends, and he remembers with bitterness her opposition to the girlfriends he might have married. On his way to say a prayer for her, through a street of depressingly similar suburban bungalows, he's arrested by the sight of a woman sitting reading by her fireside, "very dark, a western type, a Spanish-Galway type, a bit heavy" (*CS*, 1100). The feeling that arrests him is neither love nor lust, but it is enough to bring him back to the conveniently uncurtained "picture" window on successive Sundays, until he finally summons up the courage to meet the woman of his picture in the flesh.

He poses as what he is, a dealer of antiques, and gains admittance by the bold assertion that there must be something of value in the house. In fact, there isn't. The woman, Mrs. Maisie Benson, is conveniently enough a widow, but Bertie turns instinctively to the window, through which the lonely street he came in from seems infinitely more attractive. "He turned to look at her uncertainly—like a painter turning from easel to model, from model to easel, wondering which was the concoction and which was the truth" (*CS*, 1105). O'Faolain is playing quite explicitly with this theme: Bertie has entered his fantasy—and wants out.

But there's a mirror, which turns out to be a genuine antique. He bargains with her image in the glass, beholds the two of them framed, imagines himself in her life, like a more cautious Alice. She refuses to part with her mirror; in fact, she tells him, "that is not a mirror. It is a picture. The day my husband bought it we stood side by side and he said . . . 'we're not a bad looking pair'" (*CS*, 1106). Bertie steps out of the picture of his future life with Mrs. Benson and takes a cordial leave of her, believing himself saved. Of course, he's back again the following lonesome Sunday, puzzling over his conundrum: "Why does this bloody room never look the same inside and outside?" (*CS*, 1108). He decides that it could be tolerable if it were "tarted up a bit" and makes a new play for the mirror. She's a dressmaker, and the antique mirror reflects only the top half of her clients; if she'll allow him to display it temporarily in his showrooms, he will give her a full-length mirror in its place. She consents, though she's not without her suspicions. His next step is to ask if she'll consent to display some of *his* antiques in *her* house by way of advertisement for his business. Little by little her irredeemably middle-class furniture is replaced by a mélange of period pieces, and Bertie worms his way into an antechamber of his dressmaker's heart. She doesn't give in without a struggle, suspecting perhaps that it is the woman in the picture or the mirror he's after rather than the woman in the flesh. O'Faolain speculates easily about the possible causes of her final capitulation in a manner that invites us to pick and choose: was she fed up with being a dressmaker? Ambitious for her daughter? Just plain tired?

These characters have their requisite histories and idiosyncrasies, but none of this detail matters very much beside O'Faolain's preoccupation with his theme. The match, of course, is a disaster. Bertie understands it as pure accident; just about any one of the other bungalows in this god-forsaken suburb would have provided him with a more tranquil haven, instead of which he must pack his bags and move, to be on the outside looking in again. Maddeningly down to earth, she protests that the same thing is happening day after day in all those other bungalows that appear to him to harbor bliss. "You bitch!" he snaps in parting. "You broke my heart. I thought you were perfect" (*CS*, 1114). When apparently realistic characters are made to utter such lines as these, we need to be sustained by a sense of a design that transcends realism. And so we are not surprised to find that the story has come full circle, that it starts over with virtually the same words as the opening paragraph, the same character of the lonely pathetic Bertie, the same predicament. This time, of course, he remembers his deserted wife and finds her sitting by her window as before, still reading, still drinking tea. The words with which she greets him when she opens the door to him are the very words of the fantasy he had created around her before his intrusion into her world. Predictably, he's drawn to the window. The occasion is also an anniversary—of their wedding. The antique mirror is back in her workroom; she reminds him that he has not delivered the full-length mirror that was his part of the bargain, and he renews his promise. A new cycle of Sunday visits commences.

O'Faolain could have left it at this, implying repeated cycles (or infinitely receding images in facing mirrors?), until old age, death, or indifference eliminates the tension, but he's not interested in the resolution of Bertie's conflict in realistic terms. What interests him here is symmetry and the manipulation of images. Bertie finally yields to Maisie's repeated requests and arrives at the door with the big mirror. Unfortunately, it won't fit through the door. After much effort, they prop it against the hedge, and Maisie makes hot toddies for Bertie and his perspiring assistant. Resolving never to set foot in the house again, Bertie moves to the window and looks out at the mirror: "And, behold, it was glowing with the rosiness of the window and the three of them out there looking in at themselves from under the falling night and the wilderness of stars over town and sea, a vision so unlikely, disturbing, appealing, inviting, promising, demanding, enlisting that he swept her to him and held her so long, so close, so tight that the next he heard was the pink-and-blue van driving away down the avenue (*CS*, 1117). And that's it! Bertie is cured of his complex: all he has to do is leave the mirror in the front garden, so that whenever he's fatally attracted to the prospect of the window, the mirror will reflect his longing back into the cosy confines of Maisie's bungalow. There's no point in asking what the mirror symbolizes because it's obvious—and anyway O'Faolain does not intend us to subject his symbols to heavy-handed interpretation. If there's a note of uncertainty in the litany of adjectives with which he attempts to describe

Bertie's vision, this is because the neat schematic ending and untidy incorrigible Bertie don't quite jive. But we know all we need to know. Bertie *is* incorrigible, and only such an absurd and unlikely conclusion could make him change his spots. The point is to enjoy this schematic representation of his predicament. The story is reminiscent of some of John Cheever's deft satires of middle-class life in American suburbia, such as "The Enormous Radio" or "The Swimmer". O'Faolain doesn't go quite as far as Cheever, whose surreal radio admits the furtive listener to the private lives of her neighbors; Bertie does not see Maisie and her former husband when he looks in the mirror. But O'Faolain is exploring new ground, stretching the bounds of his own realism—and having some fun in the process.

There is more experimentation in "Murder at Cobbler's Hulk," a story from the same collection. An anonymous narrator encounters a retired travel agent living in an abandoned railway carriage overlooking a desolate beach outside Dublin. Two accounts of these meetings with Mr. Bodkin in the voice of the narrator frame a third-person description of Bodkin's relationship with a brother and sister living in a nearby cottage and with an English Lady come in pursuit of her maid and her husband's chauffeur (who doubles as her lover). Bodkin frustrates the English woman's design to bring his friends back to England with her—and she drowns herself on his beach. It transpires that the narrator has extrapolated from the newspaper account of the inquest in order to imagine Bodkin's relations with the deceased. He describes his story as "four fifths inference and one fifth imagination" and insists that it is "essentially true" (*CS*, 1127).

The narrator first encounters Bodkin on the platform of an abandoned railway station, "bowler-hatted, clad, in spite of the warmth of the day, in a well-brushed blue chesterfield with concealed buttons and a neatly tailored velvet half collar that was the height of fashion in the Twenties" (*CS*, 1118–19). Bodkin reveals himself as an elderly eccentric, a recluse who has scarcely lived. He has no family, no friends, no commitments. Civil war in Ireland and World Wars in Europe have made little impression on him. He has never traveled. He claims he is perfectly content, sleeps well, and dreams of his mother. The narrator affects to believe him and leaves him to his fate. But the episode concludes with an ominous assertion reminiscent of detective fiction: "He had, however, one friend" (*CS*, 1125).

There follows the narrator's imaginative description of Bodkin's friend, one Mary Condor, "a woman of about thirty-five or forty, midway between plain and good-looking, red-cheeked, buxom, blue-eyed, eagerly welcoming" (*CS*, 1126). Mary is newly returned from England and occupied with looking after her aged mother and keeping house for her brother, but she welcomes Bodkin as a neighbor and he visits the family each evening. It's all perfectly harmless, but Bodkin has made his first and only woman friend of his life and his happiness is complete.

Enter Lady Dobson, an English aristocrat a little the worse for wear. She encounters Bodkin sitting outside his carriage and shatters his peace of mind. Bodkin disapproves of her before she opens her mouth—her tinted eyelids, her scented cigarettes, her Jaguar car with *corps diplomatique* plates—but when she tries to enlist his help in persuading Mary to return to England, he hardens his heart against her. He talks to Mary, who is appropriately respectful of her former employer, but reveals that her brother is "dying of the lonesome" (*CS*, 1131). Why? Bodkin does a little snooping around in the dark and stumbles upon an assignation between the brother and m'lady. The very thought of it unnerves him; he's plagued by "lascivious imaginings" and rises from his bed next day "with the eyes of a saint wakened from dreams of sin" (*CS*, 1132).

Bodkin sees his happiness and Mary's threatened by the English adulteress and decides to take a hand in the game. He leaves a warning note for the brother and intercepts a note from the impatient Lady Dobson: "If I do not see you tomorrow night, I will throw myself into the sea. I adore you. Connie" (*CS*, 1133). There is a final encounter between the rivals on the deserted platform, in which Bodkin insinuates that Mary Condor's brother has found himself a local girl. Exit Lady Dobson, distraught. At this point the story assumes the manner of a newspaper report, with extracts from Bodkin's testimony at the inquest. The narrator then returns, visits Bodkin, and begins to probe him for information about the incident. Bodkin is uncharacteristically close-mouthed. The narrator discovers some minor inconsistencies in his story and is convinced that the man is lying. Bodkin warns him about swimming on the beach: "There are currents. The beach shelves sharply. Three yards out and the gravel slides from under your feet. And nobody to hear you if you shout for help" (*CS*, 1139). In the tradition of eminent detectives, the narrator devises a test. He stands on the beach, out of sight of Bodkin's railway carriage, and calls for help. Bodkin falls for it: "his small, dark figure rose furtively behind the dunes. When he saw me, he disappeared" (*CS*, 1139).

This is the last line of the story, and O'Faolain intends to leave us with a number of questions. Did Bodkin "murder" Lady Dobson by his intervention in her affair with Mary Condor's brother? Did he drive her to suicide? Or did he play a more active and sinister role in her untimely demise? We realize too that the body of the story—Bodkin's friendship with Mary and his intrigue—has evolved out of the account of the inquest the narrator reads in his newspaper. The narrator then is both detective and artist, extrapolating from data to produce and test a hypothesis, imaginatively exploring a psyche, fleshing out Bodkin's reaction to Mary's hospitality and recreating the effect of his encounter with Lady Dobson on his character.

The idea is an interesting one, but the execution leaves a little to be desired. There's not quite enough flesh to Bodkin's friendship with Mary to justify his subsequent behavior as the narrator has imagined it, and Lady Dobson's antagonism toward Bodkin seems to imply an imaginative faculty almost as active as the narrator's. And the conclusion is overdetermined, as they say in the trade. On the face of it, there's no mystery about what happened. The unfortunate Lady Dobson has sworn to drown herself if the brother doesn't show up to comfort her, and this is just what happens; we understand "murder" in a figurative sense. But in the final episode, O'Faolain complicates matters by hinting at what he has already apparently disclosed. Bodkin has not told the whole truth at the inquest, but surely his intention is to assuage his private guilt rather than to conceal a punishable offense? It doesn't particularly matter. O'Faolain is pouring old wine into new bottles, and we discover in Bodkin echoes of other eccentric and ineffectual male characters like the gloomy Hanafan of "Admiring the Scenery" or Lenihan of "A Born Genius." The women in the story, like most of O'Faolain's women, are strong (Mary) and dangerous (Lady Dobson). In spite of a sinister touch (that may or may not be purely in the mind of the narrator), Bodkin is a pathetic creature. In O'Faolain's world, women are the source of all action and reaction.

A Tiller of Ancient Soil

In looking back on his life at the age of 62, O'Faolain writes: "By the end of the Civil War life had presented itself to me, forever, under the form of a number of ineluctable challenges, or experiences, densely compressed into the one word, Ireland . . . We all make only one basic experiment with life. Everything else is tangential to it. I am impaled on one green corner of the universe" (*VM*, 219–20). This is to acknowledge his profound attachment to Ireland and his commitment to working, in situ, with Irish problems. The fundamental problem of the Irish writer, unhappy and at home, is whether he can "keep sweet about his material . . . The conflicts are all right, they are useful, they are part of living, so long as you can use them, for as long as you can keep your sense of humor, keep your distance, your focus, keep sweet" (*VM*, 367). This is O'Faolain's achievement, that he has managed to steer a middle course between estrangement and anger, between the obsessed exile of Joyce and the discontented inertia of Flann O'Brien. His strategy has perhaps been complemented by his sense of what is suitable material for art. According to O'Faolain, the present cannot be turned into art because it is too close at hand. The artist must draw his inspiration from the past, from the imposition of form upon memory. Throughout his long career, O'Faolain remains at bottom remarkably faithful to his original sources, to the Irish tradition, to the forms of oral storytelling, to the countryside and customs of Ireland: "If once the boy within us ceases to speak to the man who enfolds him, the shape of life is broken and there is, literally, no more to be said. I think that if my life has had any shape it is this. I have gone on listening and remembering. It is your shape, O, my youth, O my country" (*VM*, 374).

In "A Present from Clonmacnois," with which the *Collected Stories* closes, a young poet and an elderly scholar visit the ruined medieval monastery of Clonmacnois, a site the scholar describes as "one of the sacred places of Ireland" (*CS*, 1297). The poet cannot make anything of it. For him the past is too remote to be felt: "The bridge is down" (*CS*, 1297), as he puts it. But in the process of reading the translation of a series of tedious quatrains in Old Irish sent him by the scholar, he comes

112

upon a couple of verses of real poetry—and in a flash a connection has been made between his own childhood and the world of an obscure and pious monk. He essays his own translation and shows it to the scholar, who reddens the poet's ears with his praise. When the poet has recovered his composure, he is able to reflect that far from being an isolated egoistic creator, he is part of a tradition; through his translation a connection has been established with the distant past: "his pride in his poem evaporated into the thought that everything created is recreated, that it takes many generations to write a poem, many lives, many grass-grown ruins . . . The artist is a mere tiller of ancient soil" (*CS*, 1304).

This little nugget of wisdom is perhaps the end result of O'Faolain's life-long search of the personal and historical past. He has differentiated between what may be salvaged of Old Ireland and what must be left behind. As a young man, he hoped for a modern Ireland that drew its inspiration from the past, for a quality of life informed by tradition, for a direct and robust connection. He saw the desire for a modern industrialized country destroy the possibility of this connection, and as it did so, he turned inward, looking to his personal vision of the past as a source of artistic inspiration. He seems to find now that continuity of tradition is not simply a question of preserving a language or establishing an archaeological society or protecting historic buildings. The past is always with us. It is beyond our ken, but we have the possibility of making contact with it at moments of artistic or mystical intensity, the same "moments of awareness" O'Faolain has tried to make the essence of his stories. One must be grateful for such moments, in life and in art. O'Faolain's final note is one not of lament but of gratitude.

Notes to Part 1

1. Denis Donoghue, "Ireland and Its Discontents," *New York Times* 10 October 1983, sec. 7, p. 11, col. 1.

2. Sean O'Faolain, "A Portrait of the Artist as an Old Man," *Irish University Review* 6, 1 (Spring 1976), 18.

3. Declan Kilberd, "Storytelling: The Gaelic Tradition," *The Irish Short Story*, ed. Patrick Rafroidi and Terence Brown (Atlantic Highlands: Humanities Press, 1979), 15.

4. John Hildebidle, *Five Irish Writers* (Cambridge, MA: Harvard University Press, 1989), 168; hereafter cited in the text as Hildebidle.

5. Sean O'Faolain, *The Short Story* (New York: Devin-Adair, 1951). Further references in this volume will be parenthetical (*TSS*).

6. Richard Bonaccorso, *Sean O'Faolain's Irish Vision* (Albany, NY: State University of New York Press, 1987), 111–12; hereafter cited in the text as Bonaccorso.

7. Sean O'Faolain, *Vive Moi!* (Boston: Little, Brown, 1964). Further references in this volume will be parenthetical (*VM*).

8. All references are to the text of *The Collected Short Stories of Sean O'Faolain* (Boston: Atlantic-Little Brown, 1983). Further references in this volume will be parenthetical (*CS*).

9. *Stories by Frank O'Connor* (New York: Vintage, 1956), 16.

10. J. S. Rippier, *The Short Stories of Sean O'Faolain* (Gerrards Cross: Colin Smythe, 1976) 35; hereafter cited in the text as Rippier.

11. George Moore, *The Untilled Field* (London: Unwin, 1903), 173.

12. Paul Doyle, *Sean O'Faolain* (New York: Twayne, 1968), 129.

13. Richard Diers, *On Writing: An Interview with Sean O'Faolain*, Mademoiselle, LVI (March 1963), 151.

14. Anton Chekhov, *Peasants and Other Stories*, ed. Edmund Wilson (Doubleday: New York, 1956); IX.

15. Maurice Harmon, *Sean O'Faolain* (Notre Dame: University of Notre Dame Press, 1966), 170; hereafter cited in the text as Harmon.

16. Robert Hopkins, "The Pastoral Mode of Sean O'Faolain's 'The Silence of the Valley,'" *Studies in Short Fiction 1* (Winter, 1964), 97; hereafter cited in the text as Hopkins.

17. Richard Bonaccorso, "Sean O'Faolain's Foreign Affair," *Studies in Short Fiction* 19, 2 (Spring 1982), 137; hereafter cited in the text as Bonaccorso.

Part 2

THE WRITER

Introduction

Sean O'Faolain has written extensively about the art of writing. He is fascinated by the mechanics of his craft and by the psychology of the writer, and he returns to these two subjects again and again in numerous essays and interviews. In the 1958 essay "Are You Writing a Short Story?" O'Faolain pays homage to Chekhov's method, at the same time as he reveals his own artistic predilections. Using Chekhov's story "The Chorus Girl" as an illustration, he states his preference for suggestion and compression in a short story, and for "some bright destination," a revelation toward which the action moves inexorably and imperceptibly. In the preface to the anthology *Short Stories: A Study in Pleasure* (1961), he insists that a story is important only for what it reveals about human relationships, recalling his emphasis in his own work on "moments of awareness." The effect of these pronouncements is to commit O'Faolain to a highly traditional way of working and to distance him from formal experiments.

Richard Diers' 1963 interview is of interest for O'Faolain's discussion of the roles played by the writer's intuition and personality in the creation of a distinctive style. Finally, the excerpt from O'Faolain's autobiography *Vive Moi!* contains some of his mature reflections upon the personality of the artist and artistic form; it also sheds light upon the composition of "Lilliput," one of his earliest stories.

Are You Writing a Short Story?

If I were asked to compress into one sentence the most important thing about writing short stories (I mean the most important thing technically), I would be inclined to say: "Cut the cackle and come to the 'osses." I'm afraid I would say this, however, with a certain amount of interior grin. Because I would know perfectly well that it sounds more straightforward advice than it is. Cut the cackle is easy enough. But there is nothing easy about coming to the 'osses. The 'osses are the winged 'osses of the muses. And Pegasus became a star. And as Joxer says in Sean O'Casey's play: "What *is* the stars?"

What I mean by the 'osses (or the star) of a short story is its central, fixed point that makes it shine. What I am really saying is that every short story has some bright destination and that every step into the story must imperceptibly lead towards its point of illumination. I believe the whole craft of the short story is summed up in those last half-dozen words— "that it must lead imperceptibly towards its point of illumination." With the maximum of emphasis on the word *imperceptibly*. The main fun of writing short stories, and the fun of reading them, consists in being led onwards, of leading the reader onwards to the moment of surprised pleasure when the story behind the story, the meaning behind the anecdote, the interior significance of the event, makes us utter a de-lighted "Ah!"—as when our train comes around a headland and there, in front of us, is the place to which we have been travelling on a Mystery Tour the destination of which until that moment we did not realise.

But how do you do this "imperceptibly?" How do you lead your reader on and on without his knowing where you are leading him? There are, no doubt, many ways, many devices, for holding him in suspense, of giving him hints or intimations of where the story is leading; but whatever these devices may be the one thing they must not do is to deceive, bewilder, or confuse. Unlike the detective story where we are being constantly thrown *off* the scent a short story is always trying to throw us on the scent.

From *Listener* no. 59 (1958) © 1958 *Listener*. Reprinted by permission.

Everything is to the point—that inner point of illumination, that story behind the story which is the heart of the matter on hand.

Let us have a look at some famous short story to illustrate how these generalisations work out in practice. I choose—because it happens to be a very short short story—"The Chorus Girl" by Anton Chekhov.

This is an astringent little story about a man, named Kolpakov, who had for his mistress a young woman who sang in the chorus. He is married to a pretty woman; he has a family; he is extravagant in his tastes; at the moment he has actually borrowed a quantity of money from the office and is in imminent danger of being arrested if the loss of the money is discovered. So far, a rather commonplace situation. His wife knows of his unfaithfulness, knows of the embezzlement, and all her thoughts are on how to save her home and children from ruin. She decides to try to replace the stolen money. So what does she do? She decides to plead with the chorus girl, Pasha, to give back the jewels and the other valuable presents that Kolpakov had, presumably, bestowed on her, as his mistress.

There the situation becomes more interesting. But let us halt there for a moment, imagining how anybody might hear of this incident in real life and smell a story in it, as one might guess that Chekhov heard of this incident—up to this point; perhaps not even quite as far as this point. Whether he heard of it so far or pushed it this far it is obvious that at this point it is beginning to jell as a story. Because he has now got three people involved in the same circumstances—which means a certain Unity of Character; and at the same time—which means a Unity of Time. Once they are compressed finally into some Unity of Place he has the essential elements of any short short story.

Let us see how he proceeds, from the first line, to lead this anecdote to the point of illumination which is beginning to glow at the back of his mind—a special little starlight of an idea, all his own, which illuminates for him the whole Human Comedy. I will not say just yet what this idea is, since the whole purpose of taking the story and examining it is to show how a writer of short stories does, in practice (a) cut the cackle and (b) come to the 'osses.

There is no question here about cutting the cackle right away. The story opens:

> One day when she was younger and better-looking and when her voice was stronger, Nikolay Petrovich Kolpakov, her adorer, was sitting in the outer room of her summer villa. It was intolerably hot and

stifling. Kolpakov, who had just dined and drunk a whole bottle of
inferior port, felt ill-humoured and out of sorts. Both were bored and
waiting for the heat of the day to be over in order to go for a walk.

All at once there was a sudden ring at the door. Kolpakov, who was
sitting with his coat off, in his slippers, jumped up and looked enquir-
ingly at Pasha.

"It must be the postman or one of the girls," said the singer. . . .

If we bear in mind that the reader who takes up this story for the first
time has none of the information which I have just been giving you
about it, I think we must admire the amount of relevant information
given in the opening paragraph, given indirectly, painlessly, and almost
imperceptibly. First of all: "One day when she was younger and
better-looking . . ." *Was?* A memory? Meaning that the story is being
seen and told more or less from the point of view of the as yet unnamed
"she." The words "her adorer" place the woman, quite imperceptibly.
She is not his wife. They are sitting in "the outer room of her summer
villa." It is a small villa, but still it *is* a villa, meaning that even if she is a
courtesan, she at least has a small summer villa. Her "adorers" must in
general be generous adorers.

May I now draw your attention to something of primary importance in
the technique of all story-telling: that the next sentence begins with the
name of her adorer—Kolpakov, telling us that he has just drunk a bottle
of cheap port, and is feeling in a bad humour. In other words the first
camera-shot showed us the chorus girl; the director has now drawn it
back to include the man, and then slewed it forward to indicate an empty
port bottle. That detail gives us his social status, and quite a bit more
about his self-indulgent and not very fastidious nature. A whole bottle of
port after mid-day dinner! And inferior port at that!

But hold on . . . Who provided that inferior port? And they are both
of them bored, and the day is at its zenith. Can't we just imagine how a
good film director would give us the sense of that heat, and the smell,
and the boredom? He would give it quickly, the way Chekhov does it,
with the bottle, and the man's coat off, and his feet in slippers. So much
for those two. Then, in the middle of this sexy silence and sensual
lethargy, the doorbell rings and the two figures come alive, startled,
especially the man, guiltily. "It must be the postman . . ." (surprised—
late in the day for the postman), "or one of the girls." One of *les girls*. In
those words "the girls" we have the whole set-up, which I have outlined
in my preliminary remarks about the story.

But the point I am stressing is that it is all conveyed—*conveyed*, not told, not described, not elaborated—presented to us as if a curtain had slowly risen on a stage, and with one glance and 10 words the action had begun. In four more lines Kolpakov gathers up his clothes and retires to the bedroom. Pasha opens the door, and there is a strange woman, pale, perturbed, breathing heavily as if she had run up a steep flight of stairs. "Is my husband here?" she asks. The cast of the little play is completed. The situation is set.

Very quickly Pasha is deeply affected by the tears and entreaties of this beautiful wife of her adorer. But, since the bulk of the story, as one might say the heart of the one-act play, is taken up by the dialogue between the two women, we are affected turn and turn about by the contrast between the characters of the two women: the loyalty of the wife, the warm-heartedness of the chorus girl; the contempt the wife feels for the chorus girl, the shame the girl feels in the presence of this elegant wife and mother who almost kneels before her. It is a kind of emotional game of tennis.

We wonder where the story is leading us—to admire the girl or the wife? I think we will admire the girl the more when she pulls out drawer after drawer and pours every bauble she possesses into the hands of the wife—all of them, be it noted, presents given her by other men, not by the stingy Kolpakov. The wife departs. Now for the climax. Out comes the adorer, pale and trembling.

> He clutched his head in his hands and moaned. "I shall never forgive myself for this. I shall *never* forgive myself! "Get away from me, you low creature!" he cried with repulsion, backing from Pasha. "She'd have gone down on her knees. A lady. So proud, so pure! Down on her knees, and . . . and to you; Oh, my God!"

He dresses himself and goes away. Pasha begins to wail, already regretting the little things she had given away. And besides her feelings were deeply hurt.

We have come to the 'osses of this story—and what are they? Pasha's understanding of the true nature of Kolpakov; stingy, self-indulgent, gross, tasteless, playing the hero at the end, deceiving not only two women but unmasked as a fraud who lives by deceiving himself. It is to this moment of illumination that the story has moved from the start, as we realise when we reread the story, and all through the dialogue between the women we must imagine Kolpakov listening, as we the audience are listening, to *his* life-story, exposed in about fifteen minutes, and then trying to cover up with his mock heroics about his noble wife and his own wounded conscience.

I suppose nobody has ever seen the manuscript of that story, but I could well believe that the first draft of it was twice as long. Then— cut . . . cut . . . the cackle to get to that one moment of illumination which has been glowing at the back of Chekhov's intuitive mind from the moment when he first heard the bare outline of that mocking club-fire yarn: "Did you hear what happened the other day between Pasha and Nikolay Petrovich? Well, they were both in the villa when who do you think arrived at the door?"

Chekhov would have listened, and thought, "There's a story behind that story." His job after that was to write it and cut it until there was nothing left that did not lead to the unmasking of the man, to Pasha, to us—and to himself.

It is how all stories get written—by cutting the cackle and coming to the point. A blue-pencil will do the cutting. The main thing to be sure of is that you have got a point.

Telling a Good One

Stories are not written to give either the writer or the reader *intellectual* satisfaction; although it is true that, along the way, a writer may reveal his wise knowledge of affairs, politics, places, social tensions, and the like, and we cannot fail to take incidental pleasure in this knowledge and may even profit by it. Likewise, a good writer will, like a good craftsman, display along the way what Dryden has called "those excellencies which should delight the reasonable reader"—in other words, he will display his skill—and of this also we may, and if we are critics we must, take grateful and admiring note. But, at bottom, all stories are about one thing and one thing only—human relationships—and our main interest, our main emotional satisfaction centers thereon. If this pleasure does not glow in us directly or by indirection—it glows in us by indirection even in that masterpiece about a solitary man on a desert island, *Robinson Crusoe*—then all the skill of which the cleverest craftsman is capable will become so much vainglory and virtuosity.

Having laid down this law I can come to the matter of the Good Yarn. In every story something must happen, or it is not what we call a story, however delightful it may be as a "sketch," or an "impression," or a "prose-poem," or the like. Furthermore, since all stories deal, basically, with human relationships, the something-that-happens must occur within the context of human relationships; otherwise what we get is not a story but a piece of information. For example, it is not a story if a young man takes out an automobile, drives it too fast, and crashes. It is an accident. A newspaper may report it as a "tragedy" but this is merely journalistic jargon. (James Joyce once gave an illustration of this. A young woman, in a collision between two cars, was killed by a long, thin sliver of glass which pierced her heart like a dagger. Almost inevitably the reporters played upon this "tragedy," which was patently no more than an accident.) If, however, the young man with the fast car had a violent quarrel with his girl before taking out the car we just barely might have

From *Short Stories: A Study in Pleasure*. (Boston: Little, Brown, 1961). © 1961 *Boston: Little, Brown*. Reprinted by permission.

123

the elements of a story as well as of an accident. It is more than likely that the "story" would end up as a banal formula or cliché. Young writers, I may say, seem to be drawn so often to this fast-car idea that I begin to think there must be some curious Freudian urge behind its appeal. Not, it should in fairness be added, that young writers are the only ones beset by curious Freudian urges.

It is not enough, then, to say that in every story something must happen, even when we add that this something must touch on human relationships. We have the right to expect also that the happening shall convey something interesting about human relationships.

Yet, even this does not get us very far, since it is much harder to indicate what is interesting than to indicate what is not. It is, however, safe, and maybe helpful, to say that the particular is always more interesting than the general. For instance, a "story" about two elderly married people returning to the scene of their first courtship and seeing there two youngsters, seated on the same park bench, obviously in love with one another, could not possibly be of much interest, unless, perhaps, in the hands of a writer of genius; and even then the *perhaps* would be a big one. For, while the situation is, admittedly, generally true to life, it has been so often observed that it is now another kind of banality, cliché, or formula. One could easily imagine it as the last-second ending to a sentimental movie. Nevertheless, if this generally acknowledged situation were particularized feelingly something arresting might emerge from it. For instance, Ingmar Bergman's film *Wild Strawberries* used this well-worn theme of age and youth in love, and revivified it magnificently by individualizing it.

The interesting story then begins where the formula ends, and the formula ends where the individual interest begins: that is to say, that interest which appertains to the character or behavior of one single individual and to no other in the whole word—other than by analogy or comparison. . . .

From even this much it becomes plain that for the pleasure of the Good Yarn to operate what happens in a story need not be a violent, highly dramatic, or ingenious plot or happening. To enjoy this pleasure we do not need the complicated plot of an elaborate Yarn. Indeed, instead of thinking in such terms it would be far better to think of the happening as a situation. Once we get two or three individualized people into a promising situation we cannot, if we probe deeply into it, fail to get some eloquent comment on human relationships out of it. What usually happens is that the situation explodes, or dissolves, as a result of some simple trigger-incident, when, out of the human tension between those two or three people, the main character breaks through to some sort of truth-to-self, or truth-about-self, which had up to then been hidden from him, or which he had weakly or stupidly dodged.

But it is by no means necessary, far from it, that the situation should dissolve. The character may go on dodging himself. The situation may remain, obstinate and insoluble. The only thing essential to our pleasure is that somebody must come to some sort of better realization of the sad or comic potentialities of the situation—even if it is only the reader who is enlightened by the something-that-happened inside the situation. This enlightenment will, as usual, have to do with the human relationships of clearly appreciated characters.

I have to add two things. There is no time or space inside a short story for complex characterization. But, if the situation is an eloquent one, we can, somehow or other, induce a whole personality out of the tiniest incidents within that situation, much as we can see a whole panorama, see the highest mountain in the world, through a tiny pinhole in a sheet of paper.

It follows, then, that the pleasure of being absorbed by the Good Yarn is not given by the Yarn or plot. The tale is satisfying *only for what it reveals*. It is true that the plot sometimes *seems* to give a total and complete pleasure in and for itself, and when the tale creates this illusion of total and complete pleasure let us by all means revel in it, while the effect lasts—for it will not last long. A thriller, a spy tale, a detective story gives this brief illusion. But, if after reading, say, a Mickey Spillane thriller, we wake up at three in the morning, disturbed by some worries in our private life, we are not likely to find much spiritual consolation from the memory of Mr. Spillane's plot. In such stories the pleasure ends when the Yarn ends. In better stories there lies behind and beyond the Yarn a deeper and more lasting pleasure based on what the Yarn has helped—along with other technical factors in the story—to reveal about what we call the nature of things (or people) in general, or the world-at-large, or human nature, or the human comedy, call it what you will.

It would be easy to maintain that this is not only the main function of the Yarn in a good (i.e., emotionally satisfying) story but that it is the sole function. We could do it by taking any good story with a clearcut Yarn, by summarizing the Yarn in two or three sentences, and then asking how much pleasure it, of its sole self, provides. Let us do this with the famous Maupassant story about the pearl necklace. A poor young woman borrowed a pearl necklace from a rich friend, lost it, and, without saying anything to her friend, replaced it by heavy borrowing. When, after many years of poverty, she told her friend what had happened, her friend told her that those pearls had been of no value—they had been imitation pearls. Such pleasure as we may derive from the ingenuity of this tale is as nothing compared to the experience of living *with*, by Recognition of the Familiar, and, by Identification, living *as* that pretty woman through the first dull years of her marriage; then living through her first really gay and brilliant night, wearing those (as she thought) priceless pearls; sharing her terror when she finds she has lost them; the frugal years during which she repays the loan incurred to replace the pearls; her bitter moment of discovery when she finds that all her sacrifice has been unnecessary.

How much else the tale is doing becomes evident if we should here ask, as sooner or later we must want to ask: "Is it not an odd idea of pleasure to watch the unfolding of such an unhappy story?" The answer must draw our minds to the varied nature of the gratifications afforded to us by Maupassant in this sad little story. It gratifies us to watch a young woman in the most frugal circumstances being impelled by pride and honor to redeem a pledge at all costs; to consider, ironically, what pleasure she had received from fake pearls, and how dearly she paid for that false pleasure; to be arrested at the sight of so tough a writer as Maupassant intimating thereby that love and marriage may be warmed by romantic dreams—like her dream of being a grand lady for a night— but that, when it comes to the pinch, love and marriage also call for sacrifice, courage, and endurance. Surely it is also a pleasure (the Extension of Sympathies) to have felt our experience being extended and our life-wisdom deepened by our pity and admiration for this young woman? And have we not had the satisfaction—again undeniable by experience and insupportable by reason—of sharing her terror and her tears?

All of this serves to remind us that pleasure is a widely inclusive term. In relation to the arts it does not connote a merely hedonistic satisfaction. It covers both tragedy and comedy. It includes *Oedipus Rex* and *The School for Scandal*, Wilde and Shaw, Strindberg and Mark Twain, Maugham and Salinger. The range of pleasure in the arts is as wide as each man's zest for life and his curiosity about it.

On Writing

On a visit to the University of Oklahoma, Sean O'Faolain gave an impromptu interview to Richard Diers, associate director of high school relations for the University. The greater part of that interview is excerpted here.

Q: *How great a part does intuition play in the act of writing?*

A: I think the whole process is nine-tenths intuitive. Mind you, we're using words here which have been much used, much debated. What you mean mightn't be what I mean or what somebody else means. But I take it that by "intuitive process" one means something which is not a rational or conscious process. Some might say a "psychic process" that goes on above or below the purely rational, intellectual, conscious level. In this sense, I think that writing, and indeed all artistic work, is nine-tenths intuitive, so much so that I sometimes go back over a story that I've written and look at it in astonishment and say, "Where did that come from? I have no recollection whatever of this thing happening." But on the other hand, mind you. I think that the pure hard-work practice of writing has a lot to do with the viability of this intuitive process. If a man doesn't practice at his work, just as if a dancer doesn't practice at her dancing, the artistic quality of the work is much more constrained, much more deliberate, much more *voulu*. Whereas, if she's always dancing, she does the technical things so instinctively that there is room for her purely personal artistic quality to emerge in what she's doing. To make a rude joke, somebody once said to me, "Religion is like Sex. If you don't practice it you lose it." I think this is true of art. If you don't practice it you lose it. So that although I may find in a manuscript something that surprises me and makes me wonder where it came from, I know that I am entitled to some credit for that because of the amount of technical work that I've put in, just as the dancer puts it in at the *barre*

From *Mademoiselle* 56 (March 1963). Courtesy Mademoiselle. Copyright © 1963 (renewed 1991) by The Conde Nast Publications Inc.

every morning in the studio. I have worked so that my limbs are ready to respond to my impulse.

Q: *Do you still find pleasure in writing?*

A: This is a strange business. In the first stories I wrote I watched every word. I watched every line, I wanted like Keats to "load every rift with ore," every adjective had to work, and I would rewrite sentences over and over again and read them out to myself or to my wife and say, "Isn't this good?" But at the same time I was very unselfconscious in a strange way, because the very fact I could read it out and say, "Isn't this good?" shows how naïve and unselfconscious I was being. Now I would hesitate to do this because—I don't know why. On the other hand, nowadays I don't try to deliberately write good English, if you know what I mean, or write purple English. On the contrary, I try to write it "down," to keep it quiet, so that it's a more complex procedure now, and a harder one therefore. Writing is never to me a flow in the sense in which perhaps sometimes young writers imagine it is. They possibly still have the romantic notion of the artist as a creature who is inspired, whose eyeballs are "in a fine frenzy, rolling," as he tears at the page to get it all down. I always tell them go and read those two or three central pages in Thomas Mann's *Tonio Kröger* where he talks about the artist working coldly— working *coldly*. Though of course he has an itch all the time along the nerves, a physiological desire to get something projected outside himself, almost like a woman trying to give birth to a baby. And so there is at once pain and joy and satisfaction in the whole process.

Q: *Why does a writer write, primarily?*

A: I have no doubt that there are many specious reasons why writers, or would-be writers, write: exhibitionism, desire for publicity, vanity, expression of the ego, and so on. But I think these are all specious reasons, like the desire to see one's self in print, like people who want to act because they are stage struck. These trivial vanities attach to all of us—the sillier impulses of a politician to be a politician, or of a teacher to be a teacher, or of a priest to be a priest. We can discount them. They are parts of the general *faiblesses* of human nature. I think the basic reason a writer writes is because he is a reproducing animal, he just has a physiological urge to create. It is his potency. You can't stop him if he's a real writer. If he was in prison he'd write on the walls. So there's no reason for it other than that the animal is made like that. I often say that writing is a curse that is laid upon certain men. They've got to do it.

Q: *You've heard the expression, "Style is the man." Is style an innate trait or is it acquired?*

A: I can't emphasize too much how strongly I feel that style is the man, and that the man makes his own style. I say this because I am a great believer in basic personality. Each man is born with . . . if you like, you can call it a soul, or a personality, a character, a nature, and that's *him*, that is his "himness," that is the thing that makes him different to everybody else. All sorts of things chip away at this fundamental personality or unique quality, and in the end you're left not with human beings but with what I call "Quack-quacks" who just make all the noises everybody else makes. But if a person keeps this unique thing intact, he's obviously always going to be different from other people, and therefore he must find a language which is different from other people's which is *his* native style. This is obviously true of all good writers. You can take up a story without knowing who wrote it and say, "Oh, this is an E. M. Forster." Or, "This is a Hemingway." Or, "This is a Chekhov." Meaning that this thing bears *the* mark of that man's quality and character.

Q: *Speaking in the singular voice?*

A: He speaks always in the voice which is his own voice. Forster to me is one of the purest of personalities. I think if Forster wrote you a recipe for making waffles, you'd say, "Forster!" Of course Hemingway did it deliberately, too. Yeats did it deliberately. It *is* a thing that can be learned.

Q: *Does this again go back to intuition, the thing that is right for the individual?*

A: Right for the individual, and he knows it's right for him. Faulkner has it. You may not like his style, you may think it's an abominable style, but it's necessary to him. If anybody made a character study of Faulkner's style he could start off with *Mosquitoes*, from his first little amateurish writings and see him gradually developing a style, imitating here and there, taking bits out of Joyce, probably affected by Dreiser, and so on, until finally he gets to this grandiloquent Baptist revival sort of rhetoric. He feels himself as a kind of prophet. As for how genuine all the stuff behind it is, that is the business of the critic to say. But never mind, that's Faulkner as far as Faulkner can get at Faulkner.

Q: *Did you know Faulkner?*

A: Well, to be frank, I don't like meeting writers. I have done it. I once got excited by the writings of Georges Duhamel, and I called on him. I was interested in Shaw and called on him. I called on Joyce and talked to him, and so on. I enjoyed these meetings, of course, but in general I find great writers are uninteresting to meet personally, because the writer is not the man. A man makes a writer, and the writer makes the object, it's not the man who makes the object. So if you could meet the writer when he is being a writer that would be interesting, but by the time you meet the writer he's gone back to the condition of just being the stage A of the process A-B-C: Author-Writer-Book.

Q: *You've said that the short story gives you the most pleasure to write and, at the same time, the most pain. Do you find the short story the most exacting form for you?*

A: I would say—in prose—yes. I can't compare it with poetry because I'm not a poet, but I would have thought that poetry is far more exacting than the short story. They are both compressed forms, capable of close examination technically, whereas a novel is a much looser form and hasn't given me the satisfaction at all of writing a short story. To know that a whole chapter could be taken out of a novel and hardly missed is distressing to me a craftsman, just as, when I look at a great big canvas by Tintoretto and know that if a foot had been sawn off it nobody would have observed it—this distresses me as a craftsman. This is a kind of tyranny of shape, form, and structure, which applies to the poem and to the short story alike, and this makes it not a painful process but a process one has to do painstakingly.

Q: *Must a writer be, by the very nature of his work, a creator, an editor, and a critic?*

A: I think it's not at all necessary. There are writers who have no critical faculty at all, because they can't be objective about any work, they're so wrapped up in their own way of seeing things. You put a story into their hands, and they say, "Well, of course he hasn't done this properly at all, this is the way he should have done it." Meaning, "This is the way I would have done it." They haven't any detachment or any objectivity as a rule. This is not true of all writers, but it's true of the majority of writers. . . .

Q: *Do you now read much?*

A: I don't read a great deal, no. Not any more. I don't like books at all as a matter of fact, because when you make books you get sick of them, you know, and you see through them, and you become overcritical, too. Then other people's books are the enemies of your own books in the sense that they're other personalities coming in on you. This is why I have no friends who are writers, because two writers together are like two leeches leeching. This is an inhuman, monstrous association. So I don't read a great deal. . . .

Q: *Do you keep notebooks?*

A: I don't keep notebooks, no. I don't particularly trust them.

Q: *Do you jot down phrases as they come to you?*

A: No, no. I turn on the mental tape recorder when it's needed. Automatically my hand finds the button to press for such and such a place, such and such a word. The response depends upon my talent. Some writers I know are verbally inspired, they have a vocabulary of a great width and extent and the word, the right word, comes to them easily, or *a* right word or *a* good word. I grope for the word. . . .

Q: *Do you enjoy interviews?*

A: I beg your pardon?

Q: *Do you enjoy interviews?*

A: Not particularly, no . . .

The Artist's Task

Every writer is a man with one deaf ear and one blind eye, who is possessed by a demon and unteachable by anybody but himself; a man who only half hears and half sees the world about him because for half his time he is absorbedly listening at the keyhole to his own Demon, examining with fascination his primordial Shadow. From this inner absorption comes his ruthlessness; his egoism; his readiness to make use of anybody, even his dearest and nearest, to serve his pen; his insistence on reshaping everything that he thus half sees and half hears in accord with his inner self; and his endless curiosity mingled now with sympathy, now with an almost blind hatred for other writers, who are, meantime, also eavesdropping on their own Demons and Shadows.

I do not, however, believe at all that writers are blind masses of subjectivity. On the contrary I believe that most writers have much more in common with the scientific mind than we realize. Just as every scientist seeks for the inherent order of life in some small corner of nature, surely the artist who wants to understand his whole experience as a man will seek also for an intelligent hypothesis to "explain" his small corner of human life? Hardy—Dorset, and the President of the Immortals; Jane Austen—Hampshire and Good Intentions; Mauriac—Bordeaux and Greed. Where scientist and artist radically differ is in the nature of their material, not of their pursuits. We can classify crystals. We cannot classify the endless variety of the human psyche. But the pursuit of each seems to me to come from a similar intellectual desire to find order in the seeming chaos of Life.

I have to except, of course, from this intellectual pursuit those writers who are mainly excited by what one may call the Donnybrook Fair side of life—writers who choose disorder as a theme, or the tumult of their own beings, which comes to the same thing. These one might call our Dionysiacs or anarchists. I do not deny their interest. They are unarguably a minority, though very common today, in the whole run of letters.

Yet, even including these Dionysiacs, I suggest it is a true image of both scientists and writers to see them all as a scattered procession of explorers, small as ants as compared to the world, each climbing his grassblade to view the universe, uttering triumphant cries, now called a poem, now a scientific fact, one here, one there, until the world we know gets mapped and remapped, over and over, that is to say gets invented again and again in every generation: *made up*, as Isidore Rabi put it much more forcibly than I dare to when he said: "The universe is not given to us in the form of a map or a guide. It is made up by human minds and imaginations out of slight hints which come from acute observations and the profound stratagems of experiments."

Just as the intellectual side of the artist is too often unappreciated by the layman, so is this imaginative side of the scientist. Every scientist not a hack knows that without imagination he cannot move an inch when faced by a new problem. When Newton called space the *sensorium Dei* he was talking poetry; when he used such words as *force* and *attraction* he was talking metaphors. I have even heard a scientist say that Newton was being a mystic when he used those terms, as I have seen it written by another scientist that Einstein's "unified field" theory was a pure act of faith, though no less scientific as an approach for that. Scientists are always inventing shapes of life, in the sense that Max Planck invented the life-shape of the quantum theory by a pure hunch or guess at a time when he had not a shred of evidence for assuming, that is, imagining-for-the-sake-of-the-hypothesis, that radiant energy is emitted in particles or bits, or quanta, and not, as everybody else had thought before him, in a flowing stream. The scientist who says "Let's suppose!" is at that point using the same inspiration as the storyteller who says "Let's pretend," and for the same reason—to transform chaos into meaning.

The image of the artist holding a mirror up to nature leaves out of account this transformation, by selection and invention, of the otherwise meaningless jungle of actuality. His good eye, his good ear, demon-guided, decides fastidiously, intellectually and imaginatively what, alone among all the eyes and ears of the world, he shall see and hear in the green wilderness. What saves him from the banality of seeing and hearing what everybody else has always seen and heard is his God-given infirmities. They bestow on him his own obstinate vision, which is his Self in action, making these new shapes of life. . . .

To me imaginative form in art is the outward christening, publicly witnessed, of the child born of the intimate sexual union of the intelligence and the sensibility. An artist here intelligently molds—like a potter—an outer shape to contain his sensations, or intimations, sent by his Demon, of the inner shape of life. There, again, I feel myself very close to the scientist. In one of his most interesting novels, *The Search*, C. P. Snow describes how a crystallographer seeking to define the forms and structures of some complex crystal, its internal laws, its symmetrical planes, its many intersections felt, when he at last found the formula and construed its pattern or model, an almost mystical emotion, melting his intellect as a scientist into his emotions as a man who has touched a fragment of the central orderliness of nature, a part of the design of its prime Designer. So may an artist feel who captured something of the essence of some equally tiny portion of life in the formal pattern of the substance of his picture or his tale, shaped alike by his sensibility and his intellect.

I think I have always been a romantic with a hopeless longing for classical order. A critic of my first book of stories described me as a romantic caught in the despotism of fact. It is not the same thing, but it is close to it insofar as one way of taming the despotic fact is to subject it to form. Looking at my earliest stories that were of my own world and not of the world rented to me by my begetters, this is what at once strikes and delights me.

To illustrate I must make a large descent—to that very first story that is recognizably mine: the little thing, not much more than a sketch, which AE published in the *Irish Statesman* in February 1926, and which I called "Lilliput." I wrote it as a marginal footnote to the Troubles. I had looked out of my window in Half Moon Street one evening before the curfew and seen a rude caravan, made of canvas fastened over hoops on the base of a common cart, belonging, it appeared, to a tinker-woman with two or three small children. While the rest of Cork cowered indoors from the bullets of the Black and Tans, here was this fearless wanderer from the country pitching her tent in an open street—even if it was an unfrequented side street. The incident was striking, but an incident is of itself the least part of any work of art, however modest; what counts is the light one lets fall on it to pick out the things in it that make the whole incident significant for one's Demon. What was I to do with my little incident to bring out what it meant to me? I felt it as a myth and to assert the myth gave it its title. Here was a female Gulliver among us pygmies, a wonder to our simple citizens, a creature from the wild world, a tiny scrap of my private myth of the west of Ireland as the Free Country, one of those minor goddesses who float down among common men in Homer to comfort or awe them. I then let my mind fall on one or two little

Part 3

THE CRITICS

incidents—the local priest, awed and ineffectual before this intruding pagan (*pagana*: of the country); a kind citizen bringing to the stranger his modest libations; the soldiery passing the tiny temple with respect; and the outer shape or form of night, day, night. The little story is of no weight: a brief idyll. I dally with it only because it was my first tiny success, yet showing already how through form or order I was liberated into myself, to good effect. . . .

It may have been thought that I was praising myself by saying kind words just now about that youthful sketch. In fact I do not feel that any writer deserves credit for anything he does apart from the credit due to his patience, persistence and honesty. When a writer writes something the whole man does not move; a select part of him is moved by his Demon, his essential being, his talent, a thing bestowed on him by the gods as a bonus, like beauty in a woman. It may be the larger part of him, like the submerged part of the iceberg—but how can one talk of larger or smaller in such matters? Of this only can we be certain, that his essential being is not the worldly or public part of the artist, as those words are commonly understood—a necessary distinction, since the artist must also as an artist mingle with the things of the world, observe them, be delighted with them or horrified by them, know them well, feel them intensely, before he drags them with him into his submerged factory. When he is not in his submarine factory, when he is not Proteus, he is, in the commonly accepted sense, a worldly and public man, and so, and therefore, not an artist for that time being, however long or brief the respite may be from his vocation and his Demon. In those short or long periods of respite he may be photographed, interviewed, praised, asked to sign books, given prizes, introduced to the public at large as "Mr. X, the distinguished writer," and may even—if he is fool enough—bask in it all. But he is not there as an artist. Only his shell is there, being photographed, or praised; and this shell never wrote a word or painted a stroke. I praise then, and praise only my private creature, whom I do not myself know very well, whom I am in these pages trying, for the first time, to photograph as a scientist might try to photograph the molecular construction of an apparently solid object.

This is why I have spoken of being liberated out of my Self, or into my Self: out of my public "Self," my social "Self," which my parents, my city, my teachers had leased to me as a house for the time being; into my own true Self-house, where, like the physicist or the biologist in his laboratory, I could alone hope to order, and map, and understand, and invent the nature of the world into which I had been dropped—that is, understand what I really am. It may be a hopeless hope that I pursue, likewise, in these pages.

I have to add that the essential being of the creative individual, his pure personality, is, no doubt, released also at times other than when he is about his vocation. That essential being may be released in love, with his children, when he is stirred by music, or by wine, by memories, by good talk. When he is not released his head droops in the stable. A quiet-looking brute, you would not even notice the folded wings. How many, meeting Thomas Hardy in a railway train, would have thought him a poet?

Introduction

Success came early to O'Faolain. He was encouraged by Edward Garnett, and writers like Graham Greene praised his early stories. But in spite of an international reputation, scholars working outside the field of Irish literature have been slower to take an interest in his work, and intensive critical studies of his technique are still wanting.

Graham Greene's review of *A Purse of Coppers* is remarkably prescient, given the relatively small body of work O'Faolain had produced to that point in his career. James Finn's review of *The Finest Stories* not only sums up O'Faolain's achievement, but in a perceptive analysis of "The Fur Coat" indicates the specific virtues of form and depth of insight on which that achievement rests. The more recent essays by Katherine Hanley and Robert Hopkins illustrate the sort of careful textual analysis O'Faolain's work deserves and rewards. Katherine Hanley sheds light on the development of O'Faolain's technique by grouping three stories from different collections, and Hopkins's essay sounds the allusive depths of "The Silence of the Valley," one of O'Faolain's best stories.

Harmon's *Sean O'Faolain: A Critical Introduction* is by far the best book on the subject; his treatment of O'Faolain's novels, travel writing, and biographies provides an illuminating context for his discussion of the stories. The excerpt included here deals with O'Faolain's cultivation of detachment and its effect upon his work.

Graham Greene

What was it, I wondered, that gave one a sense of immediate confidence on reading the first paragraph of the first story of Mr. O'Faolain's [*A Purse of Coppers*]? It was the same confidence one felt when one first opened *Dubliners*—the boy in the dark street looking at the window of his dying—perhaps dead—friend, Father Flynn, and murmuring to himself the word "paralysis." "It had always sounded strangely in my ears, like the word gnomon in the Euclid and the word simony in the Cathechism. But now it sounded to me like the name of some maleficent and sinful being." One was caught up into a complete and individual world of experience: the writer's whole future is in the paragraph, the priest in *Portrait of an Artist* preaching hell fire, Dedalus in the brothel quarter, *Anna Livia Plurabelle*.

So, too, with the simplest possible means Mr. O'Faolain establishes his future:

> "That's a lonely place!" said the priest suddenly. He was rubbing the carriage-window with his little finger. He pointed with the stem of his pipe through the window, and the flutter of snow and the blown steam of the engine, at the mountainy farm to his right. He might have been talking to himself, for he did not stir his head or remove his elbow from its rest. He was a skeleton of a man, and the veins of his temples bulged out like nerves. Peering I could barely see, below the pine-forest of "The Department," through the fog of the storm, a lone chapel and a farmhouse, now a tangle of black and white. Although it was the middle of the day a light shone yellow in a byre. Then the buildings swivelled and were left behind. The land was blinding.

The secret, I think, is simultaneity. The short story has not time to take our imaginations by anything but rape; it cannot begin like a novel of Scott or Hardy: "It was on a moonless night in the autumn of the year 18—that a lonely traveller was observed. . . ." In this opening paragraph of his first story of [*sic*] Mr. O'Faolain establishes simultaneously

From *Spectator* 159 (1937). © 1937 *Spectator*. Reprinted by permission.

(not one thing at a time as Mr. O'Flaherty would) the inner and outer scene—the railway carriage, a whole landscape through the steamy pane, the observer and this through—"a lonely place." It's not easy to compress all that into a few lines—to keep all your balls in the air at once. There's nothing that follows—the bitter priest silenced by his superiors describing to his chance companions the broken moral unity of the Irish countryside—that hasn't been shadowed in that paragraph.

There are a few unsuccessful stories in this book—"A Born Genius," which sprawls untidily, more novel than short story; "There's a Birdie in the Cage" which contains too much plot for so short a tale—but "A Broken World," "The Old Master," "Sinners," "Admiring the Scenery," all have the same superb grasp, the fist closed simultaneously on the particular character, his environment and the general moral background of the human mind failing always to live up to its own beliefs. The old boasting Cork librarian with his talk of Art and Civilization flinches from the public opinion he has affected to despise when the priest and the young Puritan firebrands ban the Russian ballet: the old priest in the confessional, irritated by the girl who calls him father instead of canon, exasperated by her innocent stupidity, fails in compassion. And one salutes, too in these stories an immense creative humour, as broad in speech as Joyce's gloom.

James Finn

With the publication of this volume, which contains short stories selected from three earlier books plus eight never before collected, Mr. Sean O'Faolain offers his work for an overall critical evaluation. In the familiar, personal Foreword that he contributes to this volume, Mr. O'Faolain suggests the limits of his own hopes an aspirations. "I shall be content," he writes, "if half a dozen, if even three or four of my stories that have taken thirty years to write are remembered fifty years hence." This may seem like undue humility from one whose stories have consistently won serious attention.

In a sense, it is humility, but Mr. O'Faolain is applying to his own stories very high standards indeed. His own critical judgments are informed and astringent. "I know now that four-fifths of Balzac's 60 odd

From *Commonweal* 66 (1957). © 1957 *Commonweal*. Reprinted by permission.

volumes are far from being works of genius. . . . Would all of [Stendhal] that is worth while fill a two foot shelf? Story after story by Maupassant is journeyman stuff. I can now reread only the Chekovs that I have ticked off on the contents pages." The man who makes these judgments is highly aware of the erosion that time and extended critical consideration will work upon the best of authors. He knows that stories which withstand the passage of 50 years must be of a high order. Against such standards as these, the stories in this volume deserve to be measured.

All of these stories reveal immediately the signs of their local origin. Their roots are deep in Irish soil and they could not readily be transplanted. The emphasis upon drinking, prayer and parochial attitudes—those elements which provide both material and color for so many of those stories—one could find in other countries. But only in Ireland are they given the peculiar emphasis and significance that one can see revealed here. These tones and accents Mr. O'Faolain communicates unerringly. It is his very real success here that has misled so many readers to rest satisfied with an easy, superficial judgment. Several recent reviewers have followed suit and one, with an almost primal innocence, said that "Mr. O'F. has a cannily pitched ear for the blarney on a Dublin tongue" as if he were paying Mr. O'Faolain the highest compliment.

It would be foolish to underestimate the importance of the "brogues, tempers and piety" mentioned by the same reviewer, which are the material of these stories. Mr. O'Faolain suggests something of their importance when he says that some of his tentative attempts at satire failed dismally "largely I presume—I observe it to my dismay and I confess it to my shame—because I still have much too soft a corner for the old land. For I know I may be still a besotted romantic." The author's attitude toward his subject is clearly a very real element in the selection of his material. But the material itself is not the story; it waits to be informed by art. It is the form which gives life, which enhances and illuminates and preserves. Without it the materials, however closely observed and accurately set down, will return to the interesting, undifferentiated matter from which they were drawn. An examination of one of the shortest stories in this volume, "The Fur Coat," will make clear how those familiar distinctions operate in Mr. O'Faolain's work.

Molly Maguire's husband has been promoted to a Parliamentary Secretary. He readily agrees that she deserves a fur coat. "We've had some thin times together and it's about time we had a bit of comfort in our old age." Molly is both pleased and irritated at his failure to comprehend his own offer of "the best fur coat that money can buy." She revives him from the shock of sudden knowledge that such a coat would cost a thousand guineas by saying she could get one for fifty pounds. But Molly is not satisfied with his easy generosity and her apparent victory. Some vague prompting impels her to intrude the fur coat as a topic to be considered yet again. They change sides on the need of the fur coat and Paddy, confused by the unforeseen dimensions of the problem, attempts to settle it by a coolly rational approach.

"Stop it! I told you I don't want a fur coat! And you don't want me to get a fur coat! You're too mean, that's what it is! And, like all the Irish, you have the peasant streak in you. You're all alike, every bloody wan of ye. Keep your rotten fur coat. I never wanted it." More bewildered than ever, Paddy broods over the accusation and, days later, puts a hundred and fifty pounds on his wife's dresser. Her joy is short-lived. She still wants the coat, but she can't accept it. Exactly why, she only dimly perceives herself, and she cannot explain to her husband. The reason she cannot is the true story.

On the surface this is a wry, comic story, interesting for the marital exchanges, misunderstanding, and reconciliations. But if this were all, one reading of it would satisfy most readers. But what I have termed the true story lies quite below the pleasant surface, waiting for the reader to discover it. It is as if Mr. O'Faolain had been able to envelope, to encircle the real subject, by close attention to the ostensible story. The real subject, in so far as it can be stated, is the kind of toll hard years of deprivation have taken on this woman so that she cannot freely enjoy "extravagant" pleasures. This is the kind of insight which is dearly won. It reverberates beyond this particular story, but it cannot be reduced to generalization, or "lesson." Although this story has the apparent inconclusiveness of the allegedly typical *New Yorker* story it is at the furthest remove from formula. Its end is dictated by its own form.

"The Fur Coat" is relatively simple and short, but it illustrates the way in which the materials of the apparent story are given artistic form, the extent to which the particular is transcended. Others, more complex, could as readily be mentioned. "Mother Matilda's Book" goes quite beyond Mother Matilda and her illuminated book to become an incisive study of old age. "Up the Stairs," a story told in retrospect by a highly successful Cork man, reveals how "the spirit is always broken by pity." "Lord and Master" makes more clear than does any modern conservative the very real values which can attach to even outmoded traditions, aristocratic authority and private possession of beauty.

Others in this collection, "Admiring the Scenery," "The Man Who

Invented Sin" and "Lovers of the Lake" are worthy of particular attention. There are also stories that seem to be less durable, however
entertaining their initial reading. "The Patriot," "One True Friend,"
"The Trout" and "The Confessional," for instance, reveal various
aspects of Ireland and of Mr. O'Faolain, but they do not draw one back.

When one tries to recall "great" short stories the difficulties of achievement in this form become almost dispiritingly clear. And the best seem
often, in the eyes of readers at least, to be byproducts of the author's
larger works. Mr. O'Faolain has written novels, biography, travel books
and criticism. But, however varied the merits of these works, it is as a
short story writer that he deserves to be known. There are in this volume
several stories that will not only resist the harsh passage of time but will
gain added luster. This is an achievement of which any writer can be
proud. It clearly marks Mr. O'Faolain as one of the few distinguished
short story writers of our time.

Robert H. Hopkins

In 1959 Leo Marx introduced a remarkable hypothesis on the American
writer's use of the pastoral motive to express major conflicts in our
culture between a kingdom of love and a kingdom of power, between
feeling and intellect, the organic and mechanical, and between primitivism and progress. Marx sees the pastoral not as an expression of a
primitivistic desire to escape from the complexities of civilization but
rather as an impulse to reaffirm "the need for a balance of human
experience" by mediating between the two kingdoms of force. This
hypothesis not only illuminates passages and symbols in individual
works but also demonstrates a thematic continuity extending through
seemingly disparate writers in different periods; and while Marx confines his treatment for the most part to American literature, his approach
to the pastoral can be used successfully, I think, to interpret Irish,
British, and Continental works as well.

When read in this pastoral context of tensions between primitivism
and progress, love and power, nature and civilization, Sean O'Faolain's
"The Silence of the Valley" becomes a truly great example of twentieth-

Robert H. Hopkins. "The Pastoral Mode of Sean O'Faolain's 'The Silence of the Valley.'"
Studies in Short Fiction 1 (1963–64): 93–98. Copyright 1964 by Newberry College.

century short fiction. Ireland is portrayed as perhaps the last citadel of a folk-world tradition in Western culture that is slowly being destroyed by the pressures and complexities of a civilization based on urban life, technology, and power. While rendering a richly concrete expression of this folk-world, O'Faolain simultaneously universalizes the meaning of the story so that it represents a major dilemma of Western man.

In his nonfictional studies of Ireland, O'Faolain has both admired and criticized its folk-tradition. In *The Irish: A Character Study* (New York, 1949) O'Faolain observes that Ireland has "entered into the last stage of that process of urbanisation which began when the Norman invasion sowed towns and town-life all over a mainly pastoral country" (166). It is a process resisted, however, by the Irish because they are individualists. Paradoxically, the Irish writer's central problem is to achieve aesthetic distance from the primitive Gaelic folk-world that he so much admires. In *An Irish Journey* (New York, 1943) O'Faolain writes, "Not for years and years did I get free of this heavenly bond of an ancient, lyrical, permanent, continuous, immemorial self, symbolized by the lonely mountains, the virginal lakes, the traditional language, the simple, certain, uncomplex modes of life, that world of the lost childhood of my race where I, too, became for a while eternally young" (144). O'Faolain's use of lyric prose to make us feel the "heavenly bond" of the Gaelic world while implying that it threatens the necessary objectivity of the writer parallels a major structural device in "The Silence of the Valley."

Dramatic scenes of action and dialogue function for the most part to present the spectrum of the urban world of technology through four characters from outside the valley. The narrative develops in five sections (analogous to a five-act play), each one of which consists of units of panoramic exposition followed by or interspersed with the dramatic units. In these scene-painting passages O'Faolain immortalizes the aesthetic values of the dying Irish folk-world. These "silent" lyric-prose descriptions dealing with the kingdom of nature and its indigenous human society also ironically qualify the dialogue-action units. The very structure of the story reinforces, then, the ambiguities of man's relationships with nature. If nature can get along without man, man cannot get along without nature; yet, in living off nature man is continually destroying it. The silence of the valley may be equated with nature's neutrality. Throughout the narrative, sound symbolizes man's attempt to overcome this silence. Similarly, light suggests life attempting to ward off death (darkness). Eventually every individual must succumb to death, which is the ultimate silence, darkness, and neutrality. This truism is extended to show the irreversible historical process of dying primitive cultures being superceded by more sophisticated cultures.

This sound-and-light imagery occurs in the envelope pattern of the first section: at the beginning sounds creep intermittently out of "vacancy," and at the close a lamp is lit in the hotel as the blue haze of dusk settles over the valley (288). The focus of the story is on the death, wake, and funeral of a cobbler whose skill at telling stories makes him the central symbol of the dying Gaelic folk-world. At the cobbler's cottage the visiting priest looks at a turf fire, watches "blue smoke curling up" the chimney (equivalent to the blue haze), and "for the first time in his life" becomes aware "of the silence of this moor" (290). He observes the "quiet disintegration" of the turf fire and although it is May has "a sudden poignant sensation of autumn" (290). The turf fire presents the biological paradox that living is a form of dying, a paradox reinforced when earlier the cobbler's death has been compared to going "out like a candle" (288) and when later the priest sees the five wax candles above the cobbler's body.

This entire passage with its focus on the blue smoke and silence of the fire is more than a mere literary reminiscence of Thomas Hardy's "In Time of 'The Breaking of Nations'" (quoted by O'Faolain as an epigraph to *An Irish Journey*). Behind O'Faolain's story lies a literary tradition in which the universal anonymity of the folk and the recurring rhythms of their bucolic culture synonymous with the seasonal cycle (making clock time meaningless) have been used to question the concept of progress in history. The envelope patterns of each section and the twenty-four hour cycle of the story as a whole reinforce this cyclic rhythm of the kingdom of nature. O'Faolain makes us conscious throughout not only of pastoral values but of the mode in which these values have been traditionally expressed. He uses terms of art to fix permanently, since art is timeless, the bucolic setting possibly doomed by modern civilization. In the first section the visitors "watch the *frieze* of small black cows passing slowly before the *scalloped* water, the fawny froth, the wall of mountain" (285); in the last section a "*frieze* of small black cows passed one by one, along the beach" (304) [italics mine]. O'Faolain describes the pallbearers as "a *silhouette* of six men lumbering under a coffin" (302) [italics mine].

We might rank the four visitors according to the degree to which they have departed from the kingdom of nature. On the outer end of the scale is an American soldier, "blankly handsome," from the most advanced technological civilization of man, who later in the story proposes that the hotel hang up a sign announcing meal times. It is supposedly such regimentation that he gets away from while on military leave. Next on the scale might come the "sturdy," red-haired Scotswoman in "blue slacks" representative of urban Bohemian culture and sophisticated to the point of masculinity. Her assertion that "Britain's pockets of primitiveness are her salvation" (292) precedes incongruously her gesture in drawing out a cigar case and lighting a "long Panatella." Her masculinity suggests the unsexing of woman in a modern kingdom of power; not surprisingly her obsession is the topic of birth control. Next comes the "incorrigible Celt" with pince-nez, a man of contradictions whose fanatic and intellectual interest in a Gaelic revival seems artificial. He would have "an Ireland both modern and progressive" (292) and yet one in which Gaelic predominates. Innermost on the scale would be the fat school inspector whose rapport with the priest marks him as understanding the significance of the cobbler's death.

Within the valley the tramp occupies an anomalous position. "Once a waiter on the Holyhead-Euston Express," he represents the corruption of the Gaelic tradition by catering to the tourists. He sings "Lonely I Wandered from the Scenes of My Childhood" while the visitors hear in "quizzical boredom." He is at first a stage Irishman acting a role expected by such naive outsiders as the American. The song rhapsodizing on the theme of innocence and harmony in childhood is purposely as sentimental and false as a naive belief in a perfect Gaelic folk-world existing once upon a time in a Golden Age. The depravity of human nature even in the valley is suggested by the episode in which five men leap on an eel to kill it and by the cobbler's association with Hitler (293–94). Later, however, when many of the inhabitants of the valley visit the hotel preparatory to attending the cobbler's wake, the apparently stereotyped portrayal of the drunken tramp takes on a new dimension when he breaks out singing (much to the surprise of the Celt) in Gaelic and dances in a satyric manner, reminiscent of primitive fertility rites, around a serving girl. Janus-faced, with one set of responses for visitors and another for insiders, the tramp becomes a perfect symbol of the deterioration and contradictions in the no man's land where the two kingdoms of nature and technology clash. The suggestive gestures of the tramp—"His hands expressively flicked left and right as he capered about the girl" (296)—coupled with the ribald humor of the cobbler point up the natural fecundity and sexual vitality of the folk as contrasted with the deliberate sterility (birth control) and sexlessness of an urban civilization (except for "the East End" [301]).

The priest is the intermediary between the two worlds and has the most comprehensive point of view of any character. It is the priest's awareness of the dying of the Gaelic world symbolized by the cobbler's death that sums up the central meaning of "The Silence of the Valley." In his religious vocation he serves a dual function. Under the overlay of Christian ritual remain the vestiges of Celtic ritual. The refusal of the eel to die easily—"The eel seemed immortal" (287)—not only indicates the extraordinary vitality of nature but also the eel's sacred associations. In Celtic folklore the eel and the salmon were sacred and their consumption by man would have therapeutic value. While roasting the eels at the hotel the priest is suggestive of a Druid and the eel of a primitive analogue to the Holy Eucharist: "the eel again *curved* [italics mine] as if in agony" (294). At the conclusion someone brings from "over the mountains" a salmon to the hotel (also "curved"); and after the cobbler's burial, the visitors will need the salmon's recuperative power.

The whole tragic meaning of "The Silence of the Valley" is found in the priest's awareness of the multiple meanings in the word *fall*. As in Chekhov's *The Cherry Orchard*, autumn represents the destruction of a whole social and cultural order. For the priest, *fall* also contains the paradox of mankind. As Adam and Eve lost their paradise through sinning, so modern man pays a price for his technology and civilization and loses his garden of Eden. All of the visitors have come to the organic kingdom of the valley for renewal; it is ironically the common denominator that they all need and yet that is being destroyed by their urban world. The Scotswoman's optimistic affirmation that "it will be another grand day—tomorrow" is ironically belied, or at least qualified, by her final gesture in the last line of the story: "And her eyebrows sank, very slowly, like a falling curtain" (304).

In its carefully worked out and coherently sustained symbolism, in its thematic antinomies presented through two sets of characters, and in the sheer beauty of its functional lyric prose, O'Faolain's "The Silence of the Valley" constitutes a pastoral assertion of the need for a balance of the organic and the mechanical, of primitivism and progress, and of the old order and the new. This assertion is earned, moreover, by the sombre recognition that such a pastoral balance in twentieth-century Western culture may already be well-nigh impossible. And, in this sense, the story's tragedy may well be our own.

Maurice Harmon

The disappearance of the haunted hero from O'Faolain's writing after 1941 marks an important stage in his development. His discovery of the ambiguous nature of the Irish character, worked out in three historical biographies between 1938 and 1942, brought a more balanced perspective to his stories. Instead of the one-sided formula of the sensitive, intelligent man struggling against insurmountable social conditions, he treats the idea of the ambivalent individual, who is not particularly aware that he lives in sin or in chaos. The rigorous moral tone of the priest in "A Broken World" is replaced by a more humane point of view. The result is a more tolerant and sympathetic observer, well adjusted to the conditions within which the stories occur.

In any case, the suffering characters in *Purse of Coppers* were too closely identified with the writer himself and his concept of a desirable image of life. The romantic appeal of man pitted against the impossible could also be seen with irony and humor. The new perspective is apparent in "The Man Who Invented Sin" (1944), which deals with the evils of clericalism in Irish life after the Civil War. Once again O'Faolain is faced with his vision of sinful chaos, but his treatment of the familiar subject is new and different. His narrator is detached from the events. Unlike his predecessors in *Purse of Coppers*, he is not personally affected by the change from innocence to guilt; he is not haunted by memories of happier days; nor does he stand metaphorically within his own story as a victim of clerical interference. His freedom distinguishes him. It accounts for the dispassionate, objective tone of his narrative. Instead of brooding on contemporary restrictions, he reflects on the freedoms of his youth. His indictment of Irish life since the Civil War is of only secondary importance to him; social commentary is not his main intention. In all of these he is refreshingly different from his guilt-ridden, socially oriented forebears.

The opening paragraph, recounting the liberating, unifying, and hopeful spirit of Irish life at the height of the national resurgence in the summer of 1920, is full of the transforming, rejuvenating force of that spirit:

> In our youth when we used to pour into the mountains to learn Irish, places that were lonely and silent for the rest of the year became full of gaiety during the summer months. Each day there were picnics and

From *Sean O'Faolain: A Critical Introduction*, Dublin: Wolfhound Press, 1984. © 1984 Dublin: Wolfhound Press. Reprinted by permission.

expeditions; every night there were dances, moonlight boating parties, singsongs in the cottages. The village street became a crowded promenade; its windows never went black before one in the morning; the pub was never empty. Where once you could have been utterly alone half a mile off the road, in the bog or up the mountain, you could not now be sure of privacy anywhere. If you went up the mountain to bathe naked in some tiny loch you might suddenly see a file of young students like Alpineers coming laughing down on you over the next scarp; you might turn the corner of a lonely mountain pass courting your girl and burst upon a bevy of nuns sedately singing choruses among the rocks—for every kind of teacher, laymen and women, nuns, priests, and monks were encouraged in those years to come out into the hills.

The paragraph is an overture stating the themes that are later developed and given concrete illustration. Here there is a rich celebration of naturalness. The first sentence, placing the actions in youth, gives dramatic force to the transforming spirit that accompanied the movement to the mountains. Loneliness and silence change to gaiety. There is an intensification of experience, a keenness of response, an insistence on the wonder of what took place ("Each day . . . every night"). All the details express liberation and vitality—picnics, expeditions, dances, boating, singsongs, the crowded street and pub, late nights. The theme of change from loneliness and isolation continues through the last two sentences, where it is enriched by the conjunction of dissimilar pursuits—naked bathing encounters only a laugh, courtship exists side by side with the song of the nuns. There is no sense of incongruity or impropriety, no puritanical note. All those who "pour" into the mountains are joined together by a common goal; all "were encouraged in those years" to participate in that spiritual and cultural regeneration.

After this introductory celebration of a general condition the story progresses quickly to the four main figures, all of whom are lodging in the house where the narrator has also found accommodation. Sister Magdalen is "dainty and gay and spirited," Sister Chrysostom is "a bit of a Miss Prim," Brother Virgilius has "natural ways," and Brother Magellan is "an intelligent, sensitive man" whom the narrator likes "immediately." At first they treat each other with distant formality, but their growing responsiveness to each other is projected in three separate scenes. Their formality of address yields in the first section under the pressure of argument about the proper pronunciation of Irish words. That common interest yields even further intimacy in the next section where in pursuit of an essay on autobiography they exchange memories of childhood. Virgilius and Chrysostom discover they both come from the same part of County Limerick ("she held his arm excitedly"; he speaks "in a huge childish delight"). By the end of this delicately written scene Magellan and Magdalen are standing close together ("She was dabbing her eyes with his big red handkerchief").

The third section shows them as friends, relaxed and happy in innocent, carefree pleasures. They now call each other by shorter, informal names, Jelly, Chrissy, Maggie, and Jilly; they play pitch and toss in the garden; they sing songs together around the piano. But their happiness is overshadowed by the appearance one evening of the local curate. In the upstairs room there is singing, Virgilius is beating time with an empty tankard, Jelly and Maggie are trying to waltz. It is the final moment of natural, unselfconscious pleasure. Into it steps Lispeen, the curate, whose nickname means "frog." His entry is falsely melodramatic: "The door was slashed open with a bang that made the piano hum, and there was our local curate's black barrel of a body blocking the opening." He confronts them with a suspicious and humiliating interpretation of their actions. His behavior is calculatingly dramatic and contrasts with the natural, spontaneous, unaffected quality of the monks and nuns ("he moaned. . . . He let his voice fall solemnly, even secretively. . . . He roared then. . . . His voice fell again"). "If Martin Luther could only see this," he says, viewing the singing, the dancing, the upraised tankard as evidence of evil. "To think that this kind of thing has been going on under my nose for weeks."

The effect of the curate's disapproving, puritanical mind is to intensify the demands of the religious for greater personal freedom, but now they are secretly affected by the degrading view, their consciences trouble them. A new transforming force is at work, countering the invigorating spirit of the opening paragraph. "The Serpent had come into the garden with the most wily of temptations. He had said, 'How dare you eat this apple?' And straightway they began to eat it." Clericalism breeds irresponsibility and the stifled conscience. On the last evening the nuns and monks "swallowed the last morsel of their apple." Repressing secret misgivings they join a late boating party, abandoning themselves to the beauty of the scene, the singing, the timeless peace of the lake, the knowledge that this is their final moment of such freedom before duty, routine, and city life close in upon them again. But when the party tries to land Lispeen is before them, determined to get "the name of every person on that boat!" The religious disguise themselves, all rush about the priest to give them time to escape, then all scatter. But the priest sees a nun's gimp at his feet. But even this and the possibilities it offers him for denunciation are denied. The narrator fakes a sick call for the priest and steals the gimp in his absence.

The final episode, showing the effects of Lispeen's actions and his position of power in the new Ireland, takes place 23 years later. The narrator meets Magellan, on whom the years have taken a physical toll: "he was greying, and a little stooped; and much thinner." Together they lament the passing of those days in which they all went to the mountains; now the mountains are empty and no one wants to learn the language as they did. But the change in Magellan goes deeper than physical alterations. The intelligent, sensitive monk of former years has become suspicious and uncertain of himself and of others. He no longer approves of those early days; a puritanical outlook colors his memory. "I'm not sure I altogether approve of young people going out to these places. I hope I'm not being puritanical or anything like that, but . . . well you know the sort of thing that goes on here."

Lispeen's froglike mentality has poisoned the monk's mind. Sadly, the narrator watches him "stooping his way back to his monastery in the slum." In that defeated, altered portrait lies the sad results of excessive clerical interference. Almost immediately, he encounters Lispeen, of all places, looking into a bookshop window. The conjunction of these two meetings provides a vivid, unforgettable contrast. Lispeen has come into his own; the serpent has, paradoxically, entered the garden in the likeness of the shepherd and thereby transformed it to a glowing, hellish world. He is prosperous, well-nourished, exuding charm and benevolence, but the satanic overtones are everywhere: "the sunset struck his rosy face and lit the sides of his hat so that they glowed and shone." He is without regret for what he has done; indeed there is no evidence that he realizes the evil he creates. He is unpleasantly cheery—laughs three times and beams at the narrator—as he moves through his kingdom that glows about him: "he bowed benevolently to every respectable salute along the glowing street, and, when he did, his elongated shadow waved behind him like a tail."

The story is written and developed with great clarity of design, structure, and language. Nothing is too elaborate. Progressing steadily from the fine sweep of the opening paragraph, it introduces the characters with a minimum of detail; records their growing response to each other in three varied sections; and then, after the climax of freedom, innocence, and unity of imaginative background, shows Lispeen's disruptive and corrosive effect on human nature. In the final episode the contrast of Magellan's ignoble life and Lispeen's smug insensitivity is quiet and without rancor. The narrator handles this with the same detachment and care that has characterized each separate episode. His well-balanced outlook infuses the story with a light, buoyant atmosphere in which the innocent delight of the characters blends easily with the natural beauty of the setting.

This responsiveness of man and nature is used for effect in each episode. For example, on the evening that the nuns and monks drift gently into reminiscences of childhood, "The mists lifted from the hills, and the sun began to raise gentle wisps of steam from the rocks, and the trout were leaping from a lake as blue as the patches of sky between the dissolving clouds." And on the final evening when they deliberately abandon themselves to the natural freedoms of the setting, the description of the night on the lake is evocative and haunting: "the gray mountain slowly swelled up like a ghost against the spreading moon, and the whole land became black and white . . . the white cottages shone under their tarry roofs . . . Heavy drops of phosphorescence fell from the blades." Each detail is remembered with wonder and delight, just as every incident of the story is filtered through the imagination of the narrator. And Lispeen's jarring entrance into the paradise of innocence is seen as descriptive of man's relationship with nature; they see "his shadow passing across the paling sheen of the lake."

Katherine Hanley, CSJ.

Sean O'Faolain's fondness for the short story—even were it not evident in his collections—is continually repeated in his autobiographical and critical works. He is candid about its demands, enthusiastic about its possibilities, and always alert for its raw material. One of the best introductions to O'Faolain's opinions on the short story form is the preface to *The Heat of the Sun*, his 1963 collection, in which he differentiates between story, tale, and novel. A short story, he says:

Katherine Hanley "The Short Stories of Sean O'Faolain: Theory and Practice," in *Eire-Ireland* 6, 3 (Fall 1971). Copyright 1971, Irish American Cultural Institute, 2115 Summit Ave., No. 5026, St. Paul, MN 55105. Reprinted by permission.

153

is like a child's kite, a small wonder, a brief, bright moment. It has its limitations; there are things it can do and cannot do, but, if it is good, it moves in the same elements as the largest work of art—up there, airborne. The main thing a writer of a short story wants to do is to get it off the ground as quickly as possible, hold it there, taut and tense, playing it like a fish. The reader will never know how much time was spent on getting it airborne, how often it flopped, stumbled and dragged along the ground in all those first efforts, those discarded first drafts, those false beginnings, that were cut out once it was up—so much dismissed, forgotten but necessary labour. The limits of the Short Story are apparent. It may not wander far; it has to keep close to its base-point, within the bounds of place, time, and character; it will only carry a few characters, three at least, at best not more than three; there is not time or space, for elaborate characterisation . . . and there is often no plot, nothing more than a situation, and only just enough of that to release a moment or two of drama, enough to let the wilful kite swirl, change colour, catching the winds of mood.

So the short story writer, for O'Faolain, must have an unusually keen sensitivity to ideas, an ability to snatch the one small thing and make it work. There is no room for loose writing and no quarter for the conventional and the tried; too much is at stake. The writing is hard work; no believer in frenzied inspiration, O'Faolain remarks that "half the art of writing is rewriting." Neither is the finished story to be regarded as an automatic success: "stories, like whiskey, must be allowed to mature in the cask."

Speaking of his own work, O'Faolain is equally direct and only occasionally tongue-in-cheek. He has said of the genre that it is "an emphatically personal exposition," and his own stories, particularly the early ones, appear to bear this out. Of the works in his first volume, *Midsummer Night's Madness* (1932), O'Faolain writes, "they belong to a period, my twenties. They are very romantic, as their weighted style shows." They are definitely "young" stories; their heavy dependence on romantic words like *dawn*, *dew*, *adamant*, and *dusk* and their recurring motifs of the hunted exile, the solitary thinker, the burning but impractical patriot give them an unreal quality as well. Characterized by frequent first person narration, they are involved and often passionate episodes drawn from "an experience which had left me dazed—the revolutionary period in Ireland." They are good stories, these early pieces, and it is certainly significant that O'Faolain, although commenting freely on their shortcomings, has nevertheless left them unrevised.

A Purse of Coppers, the 1937 collection, moves away from the early romanticism and into what O'Faolain terms "a certain adjustment and detachment." The glamor of the revolution has considerably diminished and there is a greater and deliberate clarity of vision. There is more pessimism in this volume as well; O'Faolain is not bitter, but into stories like "A Broken World," "A Meeting," and "Discord" he injects a darkness which makes this volume one of his most interesting. The stories tend to be neater, their structure more definite. At times, in "The Confessional," for instance, O'Faolain experiments well with humor, although in places like "Mother Matilda's Book," it is nearer pathos.

After 1949 O'Faolain widens his perspective considerably. Instead of disillusioned and groping thinkers, we get a range of human beings, some small, others magnificent, some comic, others near-tragic, who explore their surroundings and themselves and the new Ireland in which they are set. *Teresa*, the 1947 collection, contains beautifully wry satire of a self-deceived novice in religious life; a near-bitter statement of man's power to inject guilt in "The Man Who Invented Sin"; an impressionistic tone-poem in "The Silence of the Valley"; a small tragedy in "The End of a Good Man"; high comedy in "The Woman who Married Clark Gable"; and a half a dozen other excellent pieces. In *I Remember! I Remember!*, the 1961 volume, O'Faolain continues moving toward greater detachment and objectivity. That this is so not because the writer ceases to be involved in the stories: he continues to study his own surroundings and takes his art from them, following advice given him by W. B. Yeats: "You must write yourself into yourself. There is no other way." The stories play one against the other, contrasting youth and age, illusion and reality.

In 1963 O'Faolain described himself as "a romantic with a hopeless longing for classical order." It is not, I think, forcing things to suggest that early O'Faolain is predominantly romantic, with form, although always scrupulously discernible, also romantic. The author and/or narrator likes to comment and interpret and the diction is rich with adjectives. Later O'Faolain moves toward greater subtlety, toward understatement. The stories tend to be more spare (although, interestingly, several are longer as O'Faolain elaborates on plot and experiments with the more drawn-out tale). So there is, as the author notes, a development away from the romantic, emotional, and verbose and toward realism, detachment, and the compact.

Since generalizations about a writer have validity only if they can be demonstrated, it is of particular value to take three O'Faolain stories and study them one against the other to illustrate the author's development. "A Meeting," from the 1937 volume, *A Purse of Coppers*, "Passion," from the 1947 *Teresa*, and "A Touch of Autumn in the Air," from the 1959 *I Remember! I Remember!* are three stories, written approximately 10 years apart, having as subject matter the past recollected in the present. All are brief, all use the first person, all make use of a "small wonder." They are good stories, although not among those frequently studied; their lack of critical attention makes them more attractive subjects for analysis. In them we may see, I think, a progressive restraint, a movement from the carefully stated to the unsaid, from the simple to the elaborately cryptic.

"A Meeting" is a post-Revolutionary story. In the decaying village of Burnt Hill the narrator meets Sally Dunn, former messenger and intriguer in the movement. He reminisces with her about the earliest days of excitement and glamour, visits her home briefly, walks with her through the bog talking of the past and present, and realizes, as they part, that Sally's memories, however doctored and decorated, can no longer sustain her. It is a simple story, carefully restricted with its two characters; there is no plot, only the "small wonder" of the meeting and the final wonder that the "old tales" have lost their magic. Sally is settled now in apathetic domesticity, with a dentist husband and three children. Her "memories of the old days—pamphlets from Russia, poems by this rebel leader who was shot in action and that one who died on a hunger strike—" are, the narrator discovers, still in her parlor but "down on the lowest shelf behind the armchair." She is caught, unable to people her world with memories but unsuited to the post-war life of the village, rejecting golf and cards as trite and concerned about the factory to be built in the "disused barracks" (the symbolism is poignant here). She frets over modern times:

> I wonder ought we have factories spreading like that all over Ireland? We might end with cities like Manchester or Glasgow? And look at all these people making money out of it all. It's hard to tell . . .

"A Meeting" illustrates O'Faolain's statement that the stories in *A Purse of Coppers* show his own reactions "after I had more or less come out of the daze" of Revolution enthusiasm. The narrator is perfectly juxtaposed to Sally: he sees the end of the dream, although he can remember the magic it used to work on him, and he accepts the necessity of going on (it is significant that he is only visiting the village and leaves on a train at the end of the story); Sally, in contrast, is aware that the dream has ended but has no replacement and so nurses her fragments. In her yearning to prolong the bits of the old dream she begs the narrator to "meet her again, some day in Limerick," to talk again:

> We'll talk like the old days. There's so much I want to talk about! I can't remember it now. We'll talk until the cows come home! And then talk again until the cocks begin to crow! Won't we?

And the narrator, knowing, as Sally knows, that of course they never will, answers, "Of course we will!"

The story is perfectly structured. O'Faolain opens with two paragraphs on the once-prosperous town and its decay, the "broken line of shops," the barracks "crumbling to pieces." Sally Dunn and her dreams, once prosperous in romance and danger, are decayed as well. O'Faolain, though, is not content to show this truth; he must also say it. The ending of the story announces "message" with unnecessary clarity:

> We never met again. I doubt if either of us wanted it or expected it. You cannot have your memories and eat them.

The story works too hard, I think, for the reader. Everything is done for him; all the lessons are spelled out. The writing is superb, evocative and gentle, but there is too much of it.

"Passion" is less explicit. Again the theme is the past seen through the perspective of the present, although the form of this story—a sort of letter-soliloquy to an absent love—is unique in the O'Faolain collections. Here the narrator moves back twenty years to an evening spent with his uncle and aunt in Cork. He is child-observer more than participant, and the incident in which his Uncle Conny refuses his six prized Easter lilies for the child who has died, only to have them beaten down by a raging storm that night, is told with excellent dialogue and a minimum of development. The characters, Conny and the aunt, unfold through their comments, the aunt with her truisms about death—"Once we're dead we're soon forgotten"—and Conny with his pathetic possessiveness—"me poor little six Easter lilies that I reared, that I looked after as if they were me own children." And the scene, the "soft, wet night" in the warm kitchen with the fire, the card game, the child-narrator secure but puzzled by his uncle's reactions, contrasts beautifully with the storm which "sailed on the muddy water through the city" and "batters into the mud" Conny's cherished flowers.

As he did in the earlier story, the narrator recalls the incident after it has passed. Again he frames it, not this time by describing the town but by looking at far-off Dublin through the window. As before, there is a conclusion, this time more ambiguous and consequently more effective because the narrator himself experiences a sort of epiphany as he thinks of Conny's possessive love and—with a start—his own:

> Or is it, dearest one, that all passion is an unhappiness? Are we always looking forward to our joy, or thinking back on it, or so drunk with it that we cannot realize it?

The final address to the love, pleading that their meeting be soon, returns us firmly to the present. In this story O'Faolain offers the reader less and asks more of him. We are not told what to think nor are we expected, necessarily, to agree with the narrator; his questions leave the story open-ended. "Passion" is, I think, a better story than "A Meeting," less romantic and more detached.

"A Touch of Autumn in the Air," the most recent story of the three, is the longest and most cryptic. Again O'Faolain limits himself to two characters, the narrator and Daniel Cashen, owner of a blanket mill. The story is set not in a small village but in the lobby of a modern hotel, moving backward then sixty years to Cashen's childhood in "what was at that time called the Queen's County." Cashen is a successful small businessman, possessed of a considerable fortune and little human warmth, and it is he, "of all people," the story begins, who shows the narrator that "the fragments of any experience that remain in a man's memory, the bits and scraps of his ruined temple, are preserved from time not at random but by the inmost desires of his personality." It is Daniel Cashen who remembers, jogged by the casual remark that "there was a touch of autumn in the air." Cashen's memories are old and idyllic—his uncle's farm on an October morning, his young cousin Kitty Bergin, a letter from another cousin studying to be a priest, the cousin's visit to a neighbor's daughter, now Sister Fidelia. Kitty and Danny, both struck with the apparent meaninglessness of leaving the country, play at making Kitty into Sister Fidelia and finish their cutting of fern by sharing old-fashioned Conversation Lozenges and listening to "the faint honking of the wild geese called down from the North by the October moon."

What Daniel Cashen has now, 60 years later, is a large fortune and a fragmented memory of that long-ago autumn, set in motion by an old nun he sees in a bookshop, a sweets-and-toys-shop, and a faint crescent moon. And he is pained without knowing why. The narrator knows, at least in part:

> The pain in his eyes was the pain of a man who has begun to lose one of the great pleasures of life in the discovery that we can never truly remember anything at all, that we are for a great part of our lives at the mercy of uncharted currents of the heart.

He consoles Cashen by pulling him back to the present:

> "I hope the Blankets are doing well?"
> "Aha!" he cried triumphantly. "Better than ever."

The story moves into a plot of sorts at the very end as Cashen dies a week after the chance meeting and leaves his 150,000 pounds to "his relatives by birth, most of them living in what used to be called, in his boyhood, the Queen's County."

"A Touch of Autumn in the Air" requires—and repays—considerable involvement from the reader. It is, of course, a story about Daniel Cashen but it is, more importantly, a story about the time and memory and the autumn or hint of death that always surrounds memory. O'Faolain displays magnificent sensitivity by choosing for his central character the relatively unattractive and unsympathetic Cashen. He is not the mellow Irishman nor the dreamy romantic; he is simply a dry industrialist puzzled by scraps of remembrance and unable to throw them into clear focus. Because it leaves much unsaid, the story is pregnant with suggestion. Although the narrator has moralized and interpreted during the tale, he allows the ending to stand simply with Cashen's bequest to his relatives who are also tied to his memories. The story keeps a perfect tension between sadness and bitterness; there is no cynicism here, only a gentleness which would be driven out were O'Faolain to insert a message. By holding back, he delivers it perfectly.

So the three stories have moved from saying everything to suggesting everything, from statement to hint. It is also of interest to compare the function of narrator in each and then to look for a bit at O'Faolain's style.

The narrator plays an increasingly simple part in the stories. In "A

Meeting" he figures prominently, has all the answers, and makes all the judgments. In "Passion" he is a child, observing without fully comprehending but drawing conclusions years later when warmed by passion and possession of his own. In "A Touch of Autumn in the Air" he is foil to Daniel Cashen, learning from the older man's inability to learn but taught by Cashen's bequest at the end. Instead of judge and interpreter, the narrator is here humble recipient of an essential truth. He is gentler here, more likeable. In general, O'Faolain's stories follow this trend, the earlier ones featuring the first person and the later ones putting him in the shadows to observe with the reader. Several of the later stories, "In the Bosom of the Country," "Lovers of the Lake," "Before the Daystar," "£1000 for Rosebud," and "A Sweet Colleen," for instance, use straight third-person narration, thus giving O'Faolain even greater detachment and objectivity.

The O'Faolain style, careful and evocative, develops through the three stories. "A Meeting" depends heavily on similes, most of them simple ones: "the street becomes gapped like an old man's mouth," "the river was as calm as a dream," "the dog was dry as dust and in the heat it trembled like a mirage," and so throughout the story. The same technique is used in "Passion": "everything was as still as before dawn," "it was about as big as a table," "the lights of Dublin are bright as youth," "it was like hearing an old, old tune on a brass band." Similes, by making comparisons explicit for the reader, do most of the work for him; he need only read them and agree. In "A Touch of Autumn in the Air" the reader is given almost no similes (there are three, all of them strikingly original) and is asked instead to work with metaphor: "the bits and scraps of his ruined temple," "a few trivial things stuck up above the tides of forgetfulness," "the jigsaw of his youth"; "Cashen was playing archaeology with his boyhood, trying to deduce a whole self out of a few dusty shards." The writing is tighter now, and the story is the richer for the absence of the many copulative verbs which cluttered the early pieces.

O'Faolain likes to create tone through his openings. In "A Meeting" we get all the early O'Faolain words in the first few paragraphs: *melancholy, calm, dream, mossy.* "Passion" employs similar diction—*melancholy, soft, haze, weeping, dawn,* in the first two paragraphs—although here the words are more functional as the narrator points out that it is precisely these ideas which move him backward in memory. And in the opening of "A Touch of Autumn in the Air" we have only stark statement and fact, no romanticism: "It was, of all people, Daniel Cashen of Roscommon who first made me realize that the fragments of any experience that remain in a man's memory, the bits and scraps of his ruined temple, are preserved from time not at random but by the inmost desires of his personality." The tone is realistic here; although not harsh, it is not made poetic.

All of the stories begin at a point in the present, circle backward in time, and return to the present, "A Meeting" with regret and pathos, "Passion" with wonder and a certain pain, "A Touch of Autumn in the Air" with gentle clarity and humility. And perhaps these states of mind might well sum up O'Faolain's own development. It is not, let it be firmly noted, a development from bad to good or from clumsy apprentice to master craftsman. Early O'Faolain exhibits artistry just as does later O'Faolain. But a discernible movement is there and it is exciting to watch the growth of a writer through exploration and discovery and openness to the exacting demands of his craft.

Chronology

1900 Born John Francis Whelan 22 February in Cork city, Ireland, third son of Denis and Bridget Murphy Whelan.

1914 Attends Abbey Theatre performance of Lennox Robinson's *The Patriot*.

1918 Learns Gaelic in West Cork; meets Eileen Gould; changes name to Sean O'Faolain; wins scholarship to University College Cork; joins Irish Volunteers.

1919–1921 Serves in Irish Republican Army during War of Independence with Britain; friendship with Frank O'Connor.

1921 Receives B.A. in English from University College Cork.

1921–1923 Propagandist and publicity director for republican forces during Irish Civil War.

1923 Teaches at Christian Brothers school in Ennis; contributes short stories and articles to Irish periodicals.

1924 Receives B.A. in Irish from University College Cork.

1926 Recommended by Lennox Robinson and George Russell (AE) for Commonwealth Fellowship at Harvard.

1928 Marries Eileen Gould in Boston; receives M.A. in comparative philology from Harvard; publishes "Fugue" in *Hound and Horn*; encouraged by Edward Garnett; travels across United States.

1928–1929 Teaches at Boston College; returns to Ireland.

1929–1933 Teaches at St. Mary's College, Middlesex, England; writes reviews and articles for numerous periodicals.

1932 Publishes first collection *Midsummer Night Madness and Other Stories*, banned in Ireland.

1933–1942 Explores Irish character in series of biographies of Irish historical figures.

1933 Daughter Julia born; returns to Ireland to live outside

Dublin; becomes founder-member of Irish Academy of Letters; publishes well-received first novel *A Nest of Simple Folk* and *The Life Story of Eamon de Valera*, a biography of the political leader.

1934   *Constance Markievicz*, a biography.

1936   Second novel *Bird Alone*, banned in Ireland as obscene.

1937   *A Purse of Coppers: Short Stories*; edits *The Autobiography of Theobald Wolfe Tone*.

1938   Play *She Had to Do Something* produced by Abbey Theatre; *King of the Beggars: A Life of Daniel O'Connell*.

1940   Novel *Come Back to Erin*; travel book *An Irish Journey*; founds *The Bell*.

1940–1946   Edits *The Bell*; writes editorials on social and cultural issues.

1942   Biography *The Great O'Neill*.

1946   Steps down as editor of *The Bell* to devote himself to writing.

1947   *Teresa and Other Stories*; *The Irish: A Character Study*.

1948–49   Travels in Italy.

1948   *The Short Story*, a critical study.

1949   *A Summer in Italy*, travel writing.

1952   *Newman's Way*, biography.

1953   *An Autumn in Italy*; lectures at Princeton.

1957   *The Finest Stories of Sean O'Faolain; The Vanishing Hero*, criticism.

1957–1959   Director of Arts Council of Ireland.

1961   *I Remember! I Remember!*

1964   Teaches at Boston College.

1965   Autobiography *Vive Moi!*

1966   *The Heat of the Sun, Stories and Tales*; teaches at Wesleyan.

1971   *The Talking Trees and Other Stories*.

1976   *Foreign Affairs and Other Stories*.

1978   *Selected Stories of Sean O'Faolain*.

1979   Publishes *And Again?* his first novel in almost 40 years, during which he destroyed three attempts.

1980–1983   *The Collected Stories of Sean O'Faolain* published in three volumes by Constable and in one volume by Little, Brown.

1988   Receives Freedom of Cork.

1991   Dies 20 April at his home in Dublin.

Selected Bibliography

Primary Works

Short Stories

The Born Genius: A Short Story. Detroit: Schuman's, 1936.

The Collected Stories of Sean O'Faolain. London: Constable (3 vols), 1980–82;
Boston: Atlantic-Little, Brown (1 vol), 1983. In addition to all the stories in
the earlier collections, the Atlantic-Little, Brown volume contains the
following stories: "Marmalade," "From Huesca with Love and Kisses,"
"The Wings of the Dove—A Modern Sequel," "The Unlit Lamp," "One
Fair Daughter and No More," "A Present from Clonmacnois."

The Finest Stories of Sean O'Faolain. Boston: Little, Brown, 1957. Includes "Mid-
summer Night Madness," "Fugue," "The Patriot," "A Broken World,"
"The Old Master," "Sinners," "Admiring the Scenery," "A Born Genius,"
"Discord," "The Confessional," "Mother Matilda's Book," "The Man
Who Invented Sin," "Teresa," "Unholy Living and Half Dying," "Up the
Bare Stairs," "The Trout," "The Fur Coat," "The End of a Good Man,"
"The Silence of the Valley." The following are new stories: "Childybawn,"
"Lovers of the Lake," "One True Friend," "Persecution Mania," "The
Judas Touch," "The End of the Record," "Lord and Master," "An Endur-
ing Friendship."

Foreign Affairs. London and New York: Penguin, 1986. A paperback edition of
volume III of *The Collected Stories.*

Foreign Affairs and Other Stories. London: Constable, 1976; Boston: Little, Brown,
1976; Harmondsworth: Penguin, 1978. Includes "The Faithless Wife,"
"Something, Everything, Anything, Nothing," "An Inside Outside Complex," "Murder at Cobbler's Hulk," "Foreign Affairs," "Falling Rocks,
Narrowing Road, Cul-de-Sac, Stop," "How to Write a Short Story," "Lib-
erty."

The Heat of the Sun. London and New York: Penguin, 1983. A paperback edition
of volume II of *The Collected Stories* containing stories from *The Finest Stories,*
I Remember! I Remember!, and *The Heat of the Sun, Stories and Tales.*

The Heat of the Sun, Stories and Tales. Boston: Little, Brown, 1966. Includes "In the
Bosom of the Country," "Dividends," "The Heat of the Sun," "The
Human Thing," "One Man, One Boat, One Girl," "Charlie's Greek,"
"Billy Billee," "Before the Daystar," "£1000 for Rosebud," "A Sweet
Colleen."

I Remember! I Remember! Boston: Little, Brown, 1961. Includes "I Remember! I Remember!" "The Sugawn Chair," "A Shadow, Silent as a Cloud," "A Touch of Autumn in the Air," "The Younger Generation," "Love's Young Dream," "Two of a Kind," "Angels and Ministers of Grace," "One Night in Turin," "Miracles Don't Happen Twice," "No Country for Old Men."

The Man Who Invented Sin and Other Stories. New York: Devin-Adair, 1948. An American edition of *Teresa and Other Stories* with the addition of "Up the Bare Stairs" and "The Fur Coat."

Midsummer Night Madness. London and New York: Penguin, 1982. A paperback edition of volume I of *The Collected Stories* containing the stories of *Midsummer Night Madness and Other Stories, A Purse of Coppers,* and *Teresa.*

Midsummer Night Madness and Other Stories. London: Jonathan Cape, 1932. Includes "Midsummer Night Madness," "Lilliput," "Fugue," "The Small Lady," "The Bombshop," "The Death of Stevey Long," "The Patriot."

A Purse of Coppers: Short Stories. London: Jonathan Cape, 1937. Includes "A Broken World," "The Old Master," "Sinners," "Admiring the Scenery," "Egotists," "Kitty the Wren," "My Son Austin," "A Born Genius," "Sullivan's Trousers," "A Meeting," "Discord," "The Confessional," "Mother Matilda's Book," "There's a Birdie in the Cage."

Selected Stories. London: Constable, 1978; Boston: Little, Brown, 1978. Includes "The Silence of the Valley," "Lovers of the Lake," "I Remember! I Remember!," "The Sugawn Chair," "Two of a Kind, "Angels and Ministers of Grace," "In the Boston of the Country," "The Heat of the Sun," "Before the Day Star," "Passion," "Dividends," "The Talking Trees," "Feed my Lambs," "Of Sanctity and Whiskey," "The Faithless Wife," "An Inside Outside Complex," "Something, Everything, Anything, Nothing."

The Stories of Sean O'Faolain. London: Rupert Hart-Davis, 1958. The English edition of *The Finest Stories of Sean O'Faolain.*

The Talking Trees and Other Stories. Boston: Atlantic Monthly Press, 1970; London: Jonathan Cape, 1971. Includes "The Planets of the Years," "A Dead Cert," "Hymeneal," "The Talking Trees," "The Time of their Lives," "Feed my Lambs," "Our Fearful Innocence," "Brainsy," "Thieves," "Of Sanctity and Whiskey," "The Kitchen."

Teresa and Other Stories. London: Jonathan Cape, 1947. Includes "Teresa," "The Man Who Invented Sin," "Unholy Living and Half Dying," "The Silence of the Valley," "Innocence," "The Trout," "Shades of the Prison House," "The End of a Good Man," "Passion," "A Letter," "Vive la France!" "The Woman Who Married Clark Gable," "Lady Lucifer."

There's a Birdie in the Cage. London: Grayson and Grayson, 1935.

Novels

And Again? London: Constable, 1979; reprint, Penguin, 1982.
Bird Alone. London: Jonathan Cape, 1936; reprint, London: Millington, 1974; reprint, Oxford University Press, 1985.
Come Back to Erin. New York: Viking, 1940.
A Nest of Simple Folk. London: Jonathan Cape, 1933; New York: Viking, 1934.

Plays

She Had to Do Something: A Comedy in Three Acts. London: Jonathan Cape, 1938.

Autobiography, Biography, and History

Constance Markievicz. London: Cape, 1934; revised edition, London, Sphere Books, 1967.
The Great O'Neill: A Life of Hugh O'Neill, Earl of Tyrone. New York: Duell, Sloan and Pearce, 1942; reprint, Cork: Mercier Press, 1970.
The Irish: A Character Study. West Drayton: Penguin, 1947; New York: Devin-Adair, 1948; reprint, Harmondsworth: Penguin, 1980.
King of the Beggars: A Life of Daniel O'Connell. New York: Viking, 1938; most recent reprint, Dublin: Poolbeg Press, 1980.
The Life Story of Eamon de Valera. Dublin: Talbot Press, 1933; revised edition entitled *de Valera*, Harmondsworth: Penguin, 1939.
Newman's Way: The Odyssey of John Henry Newman. London: Longmans, Green, 1952.
The Story of Ireland. London: Collins, 1943.
Vive Moi! Boston: Little, Brown, 1964.

Travel Writing

An Autumn in Italy. New York: Devin-Adair, 1953; English edition entitled *South to Sicily*, London: Collins, 1953.
An Irish Journey. London: Longmans, Green, 1940.
A Summer in Italy. London: Eyre and Spottiswode, 1949.

Criticism

The Short Story. London: Collins, 1948; New York: Devin-Adair, 1951.
The Vanishing Hero: Studies in the Novelists of the Twenties. London: Eyre and Spottiswode, 1956; Boston: Little, Brown, 1957.

Other Writing

The Bancroft Library at the University of California, Berkeley, has a collection of O'Faolain material, including letters, the manuscript of a novel withheld from publication, and an unpublished volume of autobiography. Maurice Harmon's book *Sean O'Faolain: A Critical Introduction* (Dublin: Wolfhound, 1984) contains an extensive bibliography of O'Faolain's numerous articles, reviews, interviews, and stories published in periodicals. It includes some early stories and essays in Irish and O'Faolain's editorials for *The Bell*. I have listed some of O'Faolain's articles about contemporary literature and the craft of writing.

"Ah, Wisha! The Irish Novel." *Virginia Quarterly Review* 17 (Spring 1941): 265–74.

"Are You Writing a Short Story?" *The Listener* 59 (February 13, 1958): 282–83.

"Being an Irish Writer." *Commonweal* 58 (July 10, 1953): 339–41.

"The Craft of the Short Story: When is a Story not a Story." *The Bell* 7, 4 (January 1944): 337–44.

"Emancipation of Irish Writers." *Yale Review* 23 (Spring 1934): 485–503.

"Instead of Plot." *The Bell* 8, 1 (April 1944): 46–54.

"Looking Back at Writing." *The Atlantic* 198 (December 1956): 75–76.

"The Modern Novel: A Catholic Point of View." *Virginia Quarterly Review* 11 (July 1935): 339–51.

"New Directions in Irish Literature." *Bookman* 75 (September 1932): 446–48.

"New Short Stories." *The Bell* 12, 1 (April 1946): 76–80.

"A Portrait of the Artist as an Old Man." *Irish University Review* 6, 1 (Spring 1976): 10–18.

"The Problem of Style." *The Bell* 8, 4 (July 1944): 306–14.

"Provincialism and Literature." *Motley* 1, 3 (August 1939): 3–4.

"The Secret of the Short Story." *United Nations World* 3 (March 1949): 37–38.

"Significant Construction," *The Bell* 7, 6 (March 1944): 529–36.

"Some Essential Comparisons." *The Bell* 7, 5 (February 1944): 403–10.

"A Story, and a Comment." *Irish University Review* 1, 1 (Autumn 1970): 86–89.

Secondary Works

Critical Studies

Bonaccorso, Richard. *Sean O'Faolain's Irish Vision*. Albany: SUNY Press, 1987.

Doyle, Paul. *Sean O'Faolain*. New York: Twayne, 1968.

Harmon, Maurice. *Sean O'Faolain: A Critical Introduction*. Dublin: Wolfhound, 1984.

Rippier, Joseph Storey. *The Short Stories of Sean O'Faolain: A Study in Descriptive Technique*. New York: Barnes and Noble, 1976.

Articles, Reviews, Interviews, and Parts of Books

Barrett, William. Review of *I Remember! I Remember! Atlantic Monthly* 209 (Feb. 1962): 119–20.

Selected Bibliography

Bogan, Louise. Review of *A Purse of Coppers*. *Nation* 146 (9 April 1938): 417.

Bonaccorso, Richard. "Irish Elegies: Three Tales of Gougane Barra." *Eire-Ireland*, 16, 2 (Summer 1981): 134–44.

———Review of *Foreign Affairs and Other Stories*. *Eire-Ireland* 13, 2 (Summer 1978): 135–36.

———"Sean O'Faolain's Foreign Affair." *Studies in Short Fiction*. 19, 2 (Spring 1982): 163–67.

Braybrooke, Neville. "Sean O'Faolain." *Dublin Magazine* 31, 2 (April-June 1955): 22–27.

Burgess, Anthony. Review of *The Heat of the Sun, Stories and Tales. Spectator* 218 (3 Feb. 1967): 140–41.

Butler, Pierce. "Admiring the Scenery: Sean O'Faolain's Love Affair with Landscape." *Eire-Ireland* 24, 1 (Spring 1989): 66–78.

Cantwell, Robert. "Poet of the Irish Revolution." *New Republic* 98 (24 Jan. 1934): 313–14.

Craig, Patricia. Review of *The Collected Stories, Vol I. Times Literary Supplement*, 7 Nov. 1980: 1250.

———Review of *The Collected Stories, Vol II. Times Literary Supplement*, 20 Nov. 1981: 1350.

———Review of *The Collected Stories, Vol III. Times Literary Supplement*, 3 Dec. 1982: 1344.

Cowley, Malcolm. "Yeats and O'Faolain. *New Republic* 126 (15 Feb. 1939): 49–50.

Davenport, Gary T. Review of *Selected Stories, Hudson Review* 32 (Spring 1979): 143–44.

———"Sean O'Faolain's Troubles: Revolution and Provincialism in Modern Ireland." *South Atlantic Quarterly* 75 (Summer 1976): 312–22.

Dempsey, David. Review of *The Heat of the Sun, Stories and Tales. Saturday Review* 49 (15 Oct. 1966): 40–41.

———Review of *I Remember! I Remember! Saturday Review* 45 (6 Jan. 1962): 66–67.

Diers, Richard. "On Writing: An Interview with Sean O'Faolain." *Mademoiselle* 56 (March 1963): 151, 209–15.

Dillon, Eilis. "Sean O'Faolain and the Young Writer." *Irish University Review* 6 (Spring 1976): 37–44.

Donoghue, Denis. Review of *The Collected Stories. New York Times Book Review*, 30 Oct. 1983: 11, 27.

Doyle, Paul. "Chekhov in Erin." *Dublin Review* 513 (Jan. 1968): 263–68.

———"Sean O'Faolain and *The Bell*." *Eire-Ireland* 1 (Fall 1966): 58–62.

Duffy, Joseph. "A Broken World: The Finest Short Stories of Sean O'Faolain." *Irish University Review* 6 (1976): 30–36.

Finn, James. Review of *The Finest Stories. Commonweal* 66 (26 July 1957): 428–29.

Freyer, Grattan. "Change Naturally: The Fiction of O'Flaherty, O'Faolain, McGahern." *Eire-Ireland* 18, 1 (Spring 1983): 138–44.

Glendinning, Victoria. Review of *Foreign Affairs and Other Stories*. *Times Literary Supplement*, 16 April 1976: 455.

Greene, Graham. Review of *A Purse of Coppers*. Spectator 159 (3 Dec. 1937): 1014.

Gregory, Horace. Review of *The Finest Stories*. *Saturday Review* 40 (25 May 1957): 15–16.

Hanley, Katherine. "The Short Stories of Sean O'Faolain: Theory and Practice." *Eire-Ireland* 6, 3 (Fall 1971): 3–11.

Harmon, Maurice. "Sean O'Faolain." *Ireland Today* 995 (Feb. 1983): 12–16.

———. "Sean O'Faolain: 'I Have Nobody to Vote For.'" *Studies* 56, 221 (Spring 1967): 51–59.

———, ed. *Irish University Review* 6 (Spring 1976): special issue devoted to Sean O'Faolain.

Harrod, L. V. "The Ruined Temples of Sean O'Faolain." *Eire-Ireland* 9, 1 (Spring 1974): 115–19.

Hildebidle, John. *Five Irish Writers*. Cambridge: Harvard University Press, 1989: 129–72.

Hopkins, Robert H. "The Pastoral Mode of Sean O'Faolain's 'The Silence of the Valley.'" *Studies in Short Fiction* 1, 2 (Winter 1964): 93–98.

Hughes, John. Review of *The Talking Trees*. *Saturday Review* 54 (6 Feb. 1971): 30–31.

Kelleher, John V. "Irish Literature Today." *Atlantic Monthly* 175, 3 (March 1945): 70–75.

———. Review of *The Finest Stories*. *New York Times Book Review*, 12 May 1957: 5, 22.

———. Review of *The Heat of the Sun, Stories and Tales*. *New York Times Book Review*, 16 Oct. 1966: 64–66.

———. "Sean O'Faolain." *Atlantic Monthly* 199 (May 1957): 67–69.

Kennedy, Thomas E. "Sean O'Faolain's 'The Silence of the Valley.'" *Critique* (Spring 1988): 188–94.

Kilroy, James F., ed. *The Irish Short Story: A Critical History*. Boston: Twayne, 1984:

Levander, Marianne. "Sean O'Faolain, Nationalism, and the Gaelic Language." *Moderna Språk* 72, 3 (1978): 257–60.

LeMoigne, Guy. "Sean O'Faolain's Short Stories and Tales." *The Irish Short Story*. Ed. Patrick Rafroidi and Terence Brown. Atlantic Highlands: Humanities Press, 1979: 205–26.

Lubbers, Klaus. "Irish Fiction: A Mirror for Specifics." *Eire-Ireland* 20, 2 (Summer 1985): 90–104.

.yons, F. S. L. "Sean O'Faolain as Biographer." *Irish University Review* 6 (Spring 1976): 95–109.

¬auley, Robie. "Sean O'Faolain, Ireland's Youngest Writer." *Irish University Review* 6 (Spring 1976): 110–17.

McCartney, Donal. "Sean O'Faolain: A Nationalist Right Enough." *Irish University Review* 6 (Spring 1976): 73–86.

McMahon, Sean. "O My Youth, O My Country." *Eire-Ireland* 6, 3 (1971): 145–55.

Meagher E. F. Review of *The Man Who Invented Sin. Commonweal* 49 (24 Dec. 1948): 282.

Mercier, Vivian. "The Professionalism of Sean O'Faolain." *Irish University Review* 6 (Spring 1976): 45–53.

Moynahan, Julian. "God Smiles, the Priest Beams, and the Novelist Groans." *Irish University Review* 6 (Spring 1976): 19–29.

———. Review of *Foreign Affairs and Other Stories. New York Times Book Review*, 25 Jan. 1976: 6.

Murray, Michele. Review of *I Remember! I Remember! Commonweal* 75 (19 Jan. 1962): 441–42.

Nichols, Lewis. "Talk with Mr. O'Faolain." *New York Times Book Review*, 12 May 1957: 26–27.

O'Faolain, Julia. "Sean at Eighty." *London Magazine* 20 (June 1980): 18–28.

O'Faolain, Sean. "Talk with the Author." *Newsweek* 59 (8 Jan. 1962): 151, 209–15.

Paulin, Tom. Review of *Selected Stories. Encounter* 50 (June 1978): 64–66.

Pritchett, V. S. "O'Faolain's Troubles." *New Statesman* 70 (30 Aug. 1965): 219–20.

Profitt, Edward. "Glimmerings: Sean O'Faolain's 'The Trout.'" *Studies in Short Fiction* 17 (Winter 1980): 3–4.

Reynolds, Horace. Review of *A Purse of Coppers. New York Times Book Review* 20 March 1938: 6.

Sampson, Denis. "Admiring the Scenery: Sean O'Faolain's Fable of the Artist." *The Canadian Journal of Irish Studies* 3, 1 (1977): 72–79.

Saroyan, William, Review of *The Man Who Invented Sin. The Bell* 15, 1 (Oct. 1947): 33–37.

Saul, George B. "The Brief Fiction of Sean O'Faolain." *Colby Library Quarterly* 7 (1965): 69–74.

Strong, L. A. G. Review of *Midsummer Night Madness and Other Stories. Spectator* 148 (5 March 1932): 340.

Sunne, Richard. Review of *Midsummer Night Madness and Other Stories. New Statesman and Nation.* 3 (5 March 1932): 297.

Tamplin, Ronald. "Sean O'Faolain's 'Lovers of the Lake.'" *Journal of the Short Story in English* 8 (Spring 1987): 59–69.

Tenenbaum, Louis. "Two Views of the Modern Italian: D. H. Lawrence an Sean O'Faolain." *Italica* 37 (June 1960): 118–25.

Thompson, Richard J. *Everlasting Voices: Aspects of the Modern Irish Short St* Troy: Whitston, 1989: 30–61.

Tuohy, Frank. Review of *Selected Stories. Times Literary Supplement*, 24 Feb. 1978: 236.

White, Terence de Vere. "Terence de Vere White talks to Sean O'Faolain." *Irish Times*, 10 April 1976.

Wolfe, Ann F. Review of *The Man Who Invented Sin. Saturday Review* 32 (22 Jan. 1949): 17.

Index

The Author

Pierce Butler is writer-in-residence in the English Department at Bentley College, where he teaches writing and literature. He holds degrees from the National University of Ireland in Cork, Harvard University, and Northeastern University. He is the author of *A Malady*, a novel published by Co-op Books of Dublin. His stories have appeared in *Story*, *San Jose Studies*, *American Way*, and in a Joyce centenary anthology of Irish writers. He lives in Waltham, Massachusetts, with his wife, Susan.

The Editor

General Editor Gordon Weaver earned his B.A. in English at the University of Wisconsin-Milwaukee in 1961; his M.A. in English at the University of Illinois, where he studied as a Woodrow Wilson Fellow, in 1962; and his Ph.D. in English and creative writing at the University of Denver in 1970. He is author of several novels, including *Count a Lonely Cadence, Give Him a Stone, Circling Byzantium,* and most recently *The Eight Corners of the World* (1988). Many of his numerous short stories are collected in *The Entombed Man of Thule, Such Waltzing Was Not Easy, Getting Serious, Morality Play, A World Quite Round,* and *Men Who Would Be Good* (1991). Recognition of his fiction includes the St. Lawrence Award for Fiction (1973), two National Endowment for the Arts Fellowships (1974, 1989), and the O. Henry First Prize (1979). He edited *The American Short Story 1945–1980: A Critical History,* and is currently editor of *Cimarron Review.* He is professor of English at Oklahoma State University. Married, and the father of three daughters, he lives in Stillwater, Oklahoma.